Olford on SCROGGIE

Stephen Olford's Notes on
**THE SERMON OUTLINES OF
DR. GRAHAM SCROGGIE**

Olford on SCROGGIE

Stephen Olford's Notes on
**THE SERMON OUTLINES OF
DR. GRAHAM SCROGGIE**

**Stephen Olford
with E. A. Johnston**

COVER PICTURE
The identities of the front top cover picture that is from the speakers and council members of the 1952 English Keswick: from left to right: (Back Row) Rev. Wm. Still, J. Taylor Thompson, Dr. H. J. Orr-Ewing, Rev. Alan Redpath, the Bishop of Barking, Rev. G. b. Duncan, Rev. M. A. P. Wood, Preb. Colin C. Kerr, R.A. Laidlaw, (sitting) Rev. H. H. Martin, A. W. Bradley, Fred Mitchell, Rev. A. Houghton, Dr. W. Grahm Scroggie, Dr. Wilbur Smith, C. H. M. Foster, P. S. Henman. (In Front) M. Burch, Stephen Olford.

Contents

Introduction by
E. A. Johnston

My collaboration on this book began under the following circumstances. One day in Dr. Olford's office, I mentioned to him that he should consider writing a biography on his homiletical mentor Dr. W. Graham Scroggie. With that remark, Dr. Olford's eyes lit up and he led me to an adjoining room to a large box full of papers. To my amazement in the box was a treasure trove of Dr. Scroggie's hand-written personal papers (acquired by Dr. Olford).

We agreed to collaborate on the book—I would do the research by going through all the hand-written material (quite a task in itself!) and choosing sermons, notes, and outlines, and arranging them thematically and theologically. Dr. Olford's part was to write running commentary on Scroggie's messages instructing pastors and teachers how to preach them! The strength of Graham Scroggie's biblical understanding combined with Stephen Olford's preaching wisdom is a fantastic match! Dr. Olford told me that pastors (upon hearing of this book) said they would "Give their right arm for it!" Dr. Olford went to glory in 2004; his son Dr. David Olford carries on the "Olford Legacy" by teaching and preaching at the Olford Center, Union University in Memphis, TN. He has provided his following introduction and personal remarks about his father.

There is both magnificence and significance to the papers of W. Graham Scroggie. Though these sermons and collected writings are indeed a treasure trove of homiletical master-pieces, they go far deeper than just a collection of sermons and outlines for pastoral helps. Rather, they represent and capture an epoch in history that bears study. They are a *freeze frame* of Great Britain when Britain was great, chronologically comprising the period from 1911 to 1946, which includes both World Wars. These important papers are far more than just a collection of sermons for they capture a time in history in which many were not yet born and others have forgotten—a time when pulpits still had an influence upon society; a time when men wore hats and women wore gloves; when hemlines were lower and morals were higher. A time prior to the advent of television, laptops, cell phones and emails—a time long ago when society actually still had a respect for authority and feared a holy God. These writings provide for us in the 21st century, a time capsule which details a society which emerged from two World Wars far worse than it entered.

It is interesting to note that both Graham Scroggie's parents and Stephen Olford's parents were associated with the Brethren as missionaries. Being brought up in Brethren households these lads were exposed to solid Bible study and to holy living which they both reflected in their own personal ministries years later.

It is our prayer that this little volume be not only a help to pastors and teachers but also an inspiration to those who read it as they feel the passion of Dr. Scroggie and Dr. Olford for ministry. For in our day we need solid biblical teaching infused with Holy Spirit anointing! Hopefully this book will be of use to this aim. Therefore, it is only fitting that, as Stephen Olford paid tribute to his mentor Graham Scroggie with this work, that also I pay tribute to my mentor the late Stephen Olford. Both men have profoundly impacted my own life and it is my prayer that they do the same for you!

E. A. Johnston, Ph.D., D. B. S.
Fellow of the Stephen Olford Center
Union University for Biblical Preaching.

Foreword:
Dr. David L. Olford

I want to express my sincerest thanks to Dr. E. A. Johnston for his initial vision and his practical perseverance in making this unusual volume available. This was a project that Dr. Johnston undertook with my father before my father's death on August 29th, 2004. It is wonderful that this very special project has been completed and is now published. Praise the Lord!

A book in which a preacher makes comments on another preacher's messages may not be of vital interest to a large number of people. But let me share a few reasons why this volume is very special, even if it doesn't reach the top of some "best-seller" list. First of all, W. Graham Scroggie, is someone worth studying. He was a faithful servant of the Lord who preached with conviction and clarity at a critical time in British history. His pastoral and preaching ministry had a tremendous impact upon his generation. Furthermore, his writings have made significant contribution to the study of the Scriptures and to Christian growth and holiness, right up to our day. W. Graham Scroggie left his stamp upon many, including my father. Looking back on the life and times of a man greatly used of God can be a fruitful exercise in and of itself. The full "weight" of one's life and work are not known until after the individual has left time behind. It is worth learning from Scroggie's life and ministry.

I don't know how many times I heard my father give honor

and credit to Dr. Scroggie for what he learned from him, especially concerning preaching (homiletics). Lessons were learned not only "at his feet" in the classroom setting, but also from hearing him preach. Informal learning times meant a great deal to my father as well. Those interested in finding out more about what shaped my father's life and ministry will have another reason to read this book. I don't know if the word "mentor" was used often in the days when my father learned from Dr. Scroggie (I doubt it), but certainly the word would fit the incredible impact that Scroggie had on Olford.

Within these pages of "Olford on Scroggie" you will not only read about a preacher, you will read a lot of preaching material. The book presents representative examples of Scroggie's distinctive preaching materials and homiletical outlines. In addition, you will find comments and recommendations on these materials by my father. Those interested in preaching will find this material fascinating, and will gain ideas for sermon development. Scroggie had a sharp analytical mind, which engaged the Scripture at the level of the "preaching unit" as well as at the level of chapters, books, and great themes. The preacher will benefit from reading these messages, outlines, and comments, and will get a "feel" for how Scroggie thought, and how he handled the Word.

We live in a day of various preaching approaches and styles. Many do not seek to present their material in the orderly, carefully outlined style of W. Graham Scroggie. I understand that the Scripture does not tell us the exact manner or style of preaching that must be followed on every occasion. We do know that we must *"rightly divide the Word of truth"* (2 Tim. 2:15) and that we must *"preach the Word"* (2 Tim. 4:2). We do know that attention must be given to *"reading, to exhortation, to doctrine"* (1 Tim. 4:13). We do know that one's preaching ministry should *"convince, rebuke, exhort with all longsuffering and teaching"* (2 Tim. 4:2). We do have Biblical instructions and examples, and we do know the need to be filled and empowered by the Holy Spirit. But, much can be learned by studying a preacher who was or now is an excellent practitioner of the style used, and that certainly was true of Scroggie. That was true of my father as well! Even though you have to be careful comparing preaching to other activities, it certainly is important to learn from those who know what they are doing, and who do it well. To be more specific, preachers need to learn from those who preach often and preach well consistently. It shouldn't be a struggle for a speaker to come up with a decent message once in a while, but to preach consistently well with the pressures of regular ministry upon the preacher is a sign of personal discipline and divine enablement.

There are some noteworthy characteristics of Scroggie's materials that will or should challenge us. Behind the homiletical processes and patterns, you sense a commitment—to be Biblical in content, accurate in analysis, and clear in presentation. Regardless of style, the preacher has an obligation to preach the truths of the Scriptures faithfully, accurately, and clearly. How such preaching is needed in our day for the glory of God!

I believe though, that there is something more that can be gleaned from these pages. It is a "spiritual thrust." There is little preoccupation with irrelevant cultural matters, rather there is a concern for the Word of God and the walk of the Christian. These are important fundamentals in the shaping of the life of the Christian, as well as in the shaping of the ministry of a preacher. If our love of the Word and our commitment to the walk is strengthened through the reading of this volume, then this unique book will have served a valuable purpose. I know that this is the desire of Dr. Johnston, and we are praying with him toward that end.

God has chosen to use the preaching of the Word of God in the power of the Holy Spirit to accomplish His purposes of salvation and sanctification. It is a glorious honor for preachers to be instruments, vessels in the service of the King. Preachers indeed are "earthen vessels" carrying the treasure of the gospel of Christ, *that the excellence of the power may be of God and not of* [the preacher]" (2 Cor. 4:7). Both Scroggie and Olford knew these truths and wanted all the glory to go to God. They knew that the power in ministry belonged to God and that the role of the preacher was to lift high the "treasure" and let it shine in all its brilliance. To expand on this, they wanted the focus to be on the Lord Himself, the Word, the gospel of Christ, and the message to be proclaimed. Scroggie and Olford knew the humble role of the preacher, and yet at the same time the wondrous privilege of being caught up in God's great plan and "drama of redemption." We owe a debt of gratitude to Dr. Johnston for giving us an incredible opportunity to be blessed.

May we learn what God desires for us to learn as we read these pages, and then may we put our learning into living and preaching for the glory of Christ.

Dr. David L. Olford,
President Olford Ministries Intl.

Preface:
Dr. Ted S. Rendall

Edinburgh, the Athens of the North, has heard many great preachers, including Alexander Whyte, Horatius Bonar, and George Matheson. But in the twentieth century one church, Charlotte Baptist Chapel, had a succession of notable preachers whose names are known around the world. These include Joseph Kemp, W. Graham Scroggie, Sidlow Baxter, Alan Redpath and Gerald Griffiths. All were able expositors of God's Word, but W. Graham Scroggie was preeminently the Bible teacher. Each of these men published books, but no one left a printed legacy of Bible studies like that of Dr. Scroggie.

One of eight children, only three of whom lived to adulthood, W. Graham Scroggie was born of Scottish parents in 1879 at Great Malvern, England. His evangelical father, James J. Scroggie, had served with the North East Coast Mission in Aberdeenshire, Scotland, before moving to Holybourne in England. It was here that he brought his bride, Jennie, from Newburgh, north of Aberdeen. Dr. Scroggie selected incidents from his mother's diaries and published them as *The Story of a Life in the Love of God*, a moving account of the trials and triumphs of faith in God.

Since his godly parents were associated with the Brethren, the son was exposed to Bible truth at home and in church, particularly the dispensational-premillennial teaching of J. N. Darby and others, a view which he held throughout his ministry. After a few years in business, at the age of 19 he was accepted by Spurgeon's College to train for the Baptist ministry.

Dr. Scroggie served five churches: a church in Leytonstone, E. London (1899-1902); Trinity Church, Halifax, Yorkshire (1902-1905); Bethesda Free Church, Sunderland (1907-1916); Charlotte Baptist Chapel, Edinburgh, Scotland (1916-1933); and the Metropolitan Tabernacle, London (1938-1944). The years, 1933-1937, were spent in itinerant ministry in New Zealand, Australia, Tasmania, Canada and the United States. It is instructive to learn that he was dismissed from his first church because he opposed theological liberalism and from his second church because he opposed worldliness.

Before he went to Sunderland, Dr. Scroggie underwent a profound experience of meeting with God through God's Word. For two difficult years, when he was without a regular income except for occasional gifts, he gave himself unreservedly to the study of the Scriptures. During this period he laid the foundation of all his subsequent teaching and preaching of God's Word. In 1950, while giving the Bible readings at the Keswick Convention, without giving a date for the experience, he shared this testimony with his hearers:

> Can I ever forget the time, long ago, when my whole life and ministry were suddenly challenged; when it was revealed to me that I was little more than a middleman between my books and my people; when it dawned upon me that I was more anxious to be a *preacher* than to be God's *messenger*; that my master-passion was not the accomplishment of the will of God at any cost, and that my ruling motive was not the love of Christ.
>
> In that hour the edifice I had been building lay in ruins about me, and for a while all was dark despair. But "into the woods my Master came," and finding me there, in His mercy He brought me out, out into newness of life, out into fullness of service; and although I blush to think of much that lies between that hour and this, yet I gratefully bear testimony that His coming then and in that way, has been the determining factor of my life.[1]

1 The Land and Life of Rest, W. Graham Scroggie, Pickering & Inglis, London,

It is fitting that another man of God who was deeply influenced by his teaching while he was a student in London has provided commentary for this selection of the Bible outlines and sermons of Dr. Scroggie. Dr. Olford often quoted his teacher and most certainly embodied in his own preaching and teaching the passion for God's Word that he saw so clearly in Graham Scroggie.

Dr. Ted S. Rendall
Minister & Professor in Residence
Olford Ministries International
Chancellor Emeritus
Prairie Bible Institute

1950, p 86.

1
Stephen Olford
on Scroggie

It is my desire to re-introduce Dr. W. Graham Scroggie to Christendom through this personal treasury of his notes, outlines, and sermons. This way, we can place Graham Scroggie in his proper place in history for many today who are unfamiliar with his rightful reputation. My intent here, is to present him as a pastor, a preacher and a professor.

As Pastor

At the age nineteen, Scroggie entered Spurgeon's College, London, to train for the Baptist ministry. He was turned out of his first two churches because of his opposition to modernism in the one and worldliness in the other! But the experience matured him for what was to follow.

In God's timing, he was called to the pastorate at Bethesda, Sunderland, where for ten years he served with distinction. Later he was called to Charlotte Baptist Chapel, Edinburgh, where his pastoral influence and powerful expository preaching impacted the entire city. Indeed, the prestigious University of Edinburgh conferred upon him the *rare* degree of Doctor of Divinity, in recognition of his work in the Capital.

In October 1965, I had the privilege of conducting an evangelistic crusade in the famous Usher Hall for a solid month. Charlotte Chapel (the largest Baptist church in Scotland) supported the crusade with "might and main" to the glory of God and the blessing of the city. This intrigued me and made me investigate some of the reasons! Almost every observation I made pointed back to the mastery and ministry of Dr. Graham Scroggie. His Spirit anointed influence and systematic teaching and training throughout his watch, had a profound effect upon the church. It was "every member evangelism" and discipleship. He was like Charles Haddon Spurgeon in that he worked through his elders and deacons to "equip the saints for the work and ministry, for the edifying of the body of Christ" (Eph. 4:12). In fact, there were times when he and his membership rented the Usher Hall for special outreach ministry to the city! So we reaped his kind of "backing" when we came to Edinburgh in 1965.

As Preacher

My most vivid memories of Dr. Scroggie's preaching/teaching ministry was at the famous Keswick Conventions–held each year in the picturesque town of Keswick, in the English Lake District—and date back to 1875 right up to my formative years as a young theological student. He was regarded as "the foremost Keswick speaker of his day" (*Transforming Keswick*, OM Publishing, p 249). His main role was to speak at the morning "Bible Reading" sessions for fifty minutes–period! His expositions mainly in the form of book studies, were masterpieces of authentic hermeneutics, homiletics, and practical application of the great teaching on Scriptural holiness and associated subjects. His teaching on the Lordship of Christ was the most powerful treatment of this doctrine that I have ever heard. He was at least twelve times at Keswick in my time. He was, indeed a preacher/ teacher par excellence!

As Professor

It is my desire to share the significant impact he had upon me personally in terms of expository preaching. His knowledge and ability as a teaching professor are best illustrated in a Foreword he wrote to W. E. Vine's *Expository Dictionary of Biblical Words*. With professor F. F. Bruce, D. D., he maintained that "There can be no true biblical theology unless it is based upon sound biblical exegesis and there can be no sound biblical exegesis unless a firm textual and grammatical foundation have been laid for it," (*Vines Expository Dictionary of Biblical Words.* Thomas Nelson Publisher 1984). His foreword to Vine's Dictionary is sheer brilliance of scholarship!

My recollections of my homiletical mentor, Dr. Graham Scroggie, include both my testimony and tribute to a man of God, a scholar and an expositor of God's Word–who made the deepest impression on me and on my training to be a preacher. The brief introduction to this volume has already brought Dr. W. Graham Scroggie to our attention. But, his sermons and pastoral insights that follow will further endear him to you as you "read, learn, and inwardly digest" the precious truths that you will find in the pages ahead. I could write a book on the man, but four recollections must suffice.

I remember his sense of humor

This is all the more remarkable, since his gaunt face, striking mustache, piercing gray eyes, and dignified presence tended, at first, to inspire awe. In his professorial role, he earned respect and restraint from the word go. You couldn't fool about when he was teaching! And yet in no time, he became a friend, mentor, and an example to me. I could consult with him on any matter with freedom and confidence.

Yes, he could be humorous at times–even when driving home a point or principle. Bearing down on the subject of disciplined devotions (The Quiet Time), he made it clear that this tryst with God, day-by-day, was serious business. Having delivered his soul on the matter, he asked for questions. After a pause, I raised my hand. "But I don't always feel like it." There was no pause now! In a thundering voice, and piercing eyes, he nailed me with these memorable words: "Pray when you feel like it, pray when you don't feel like it, pray until you do feel like it!" That was it. Prayer has little to do with emotions to start with. It is rather a call to obedience and dependence on God. The class exploded in laughter out of sheer relief, but no one ever forgot that lesson.

He was a favorite speaker at the famous Keswick Convention in England–especially for his Bible Expositions (Readings) morning by morning. One day, I was standing with him in the speaker's lounge overlooking Lake Derwentwater. I remarked that he and I were the only Baptist speakers on the rostrum! (Most of the others were Episcopalians). He pointed to the lake and joked, "There's enough water there, my brother, to resolve that problem!" I could go on and on, but there are more important memories to share.

I remember his life of Holiness

To watch him day-by-day was a lesson in the life of holiness. Like the Shunammite woman who remarked to her husband concerning the prophet Elisha, my colleagues and I could honestly say, *"Look now, (we) know that this is a holy man of God, who passes us by regularly"* (2 Kgs. 4:9).

He was at one time, the most powerful exponent of Scriptural holiness at the Keswick Convention in England. On a number of occasions Scroggie spoke of a decisive moment, thirteen years after his conversion and two years after the commencement of his pastoral ministry (in 1899), in which the Bible and Christ came alive for him in a new way. In 1942 Scroggie told the Convention audience, "I shall never forget days of despair in my first ministry in East London." He even told his wife at that point that he would pull out of ministry. "I have no message," he agonized. "I have no power, I have no joy, and it will kill me." But when he was out walking in nearby Epping Forest, Scroggie "met with God" and became convinced that God was telling him to make a fresh resolve to put the Bible at the center of his ministry. He stated on another occasion, that he had learned many things at Spurgeon's Pastor's College in London, where he had trained, but he confessed that he had not learned at that time how to live the Christian life victoriously. Scroggie's personal story made a deep impression on Keswick in 1950 and again in 1954 when he looked back over forty-two years as a Keswick speaker. Although there was a movement, under Scroggie's influence towards Keswick becoming more of an evangelical Bible teaching event, the emphasis on spiritual transformation continued. Scroggie's teaching on Christ's Lordship proved a unifying force. (*Transforming Keswick*, OM Publishing, 2000, p 42).

I remember his use of Homiletics

He was a master of hermeneutics and homiletics. In the pages to follow the reader will see this demonstrated and illustrated. Later on I will share the *Golden Hammer* he gave me to crack open the text of the Word into component parts for clear preaching and application. This methodology has never failed me.

I remember his gift of Helpfulness

I have had many teaching professors in my time, but no one ever taught with such insight, instructiveness, and inspiration. Even when Dr. Scroggie had to be hospitalized, he invited me to come to his bedside in order to mentor me. I owe him such a debt of gratitude–right up to this very day!

Dr. Scroggie's *Golden Hammer*

It was at the Missionary Training Colony in Upper Norword, London where I first learned about Dr. Scroggie's *Golden Hammer* to open up the text of the Word. *The Golden Hammer* is as follows:

1. What is the dominating theme?
2. What are the unifying thoughts?
3. What is the motivating thrust?

Here now is the breakdown of the "Golden Hammer". Dr. Scroggie invariably started with a helpful preamble. For example, he would insist that I was to:

A. READ the passage in question–over and over again.
B. RESEARCH the passage in question–observing three principles:
   1. **The Historical Principle.** The setting or historical background. I must ask the questions—Why? When? Where? and by Whom were the words spoken? This is *important*.
   2. **The Contextual Principle.** No verse or passage of Scripture should be interpreted out of context–both the *focal and total* contexts.

3. **The Grammatical Principle.** Every effort should be made to understand precisely what the words mean as they were employed by the author–even if he is not named. All words, verbs, (tenses) pronouns, and syntax should be researched for *meaning and clarity.*

C. RELATE the passage in question. This is where the GOLDEN HAMMER was put to use! To relate a verse, or preferably a unit of Scripture to my audience, three questions need to be *asked and answered.*

1. **What is the Dominating Theme?** The Bible is so rich and full of meaning that it is possible to preach more than one sermon from the same passage or verse. So, I must be selective. To quote Dr. F. B. Meyer (a great favorite of Dr. Scroggie), "The secret of preaching is not saying seven things, but saying one thing seven times." So, I was exhorted to select my theme (subject) from the passage before me.

2. **What are the Integrating Thoughts?** Every subject or dominating theme must have supporting or qualifying evidence. In a sermon, the breakdown of this theme from *the context* constitutes the headings and subheadings of the main proposition. I need to ask, "What are the *integrating thoughts?*"

3. **What is the Motivating Thrust?** With the careful consideration of the *dominating theme* and *integrating thoughts,* I then come to the *motivating thrust,* which, in turn, becomes the *doctrine* or *challenge* of the sermon.

Let me take these questions and illustrate them briefly from a passage in Romans 1:1-17. Read these verses *carefully* and note:

A) **The Dominating Theme.** You can't read through these seventeen verses without being impressed with the recurring theme of the Gospel:

(v. 1) – **the gospel of God.**

(v. 9) – **the gospel of His Son.**

(v. 15) – **the gospel.**

(v. 16) – **the gospel of Christ (some versions just read "the gospel")**

So we see that the *dominating theme* is "the gospel."

B) **The Integrating Thoughts**. With a little study, the following thoughts emerge:
  1) **The Supremacy of the Gospel.** *"I am not ashamed of the gospel of Christ"* (v. 16). Paul is here referring to the supremacy of the **God** of the gospel–*"the gospel of God"* (v.1); the supremacy of the **gift** of the gospel–*"the gospel...is the **power of God unto salvation** to every one that believes"* (v. 16).
     a) **The Gospel Mediates Saving Power.** *"It is the power of God unto salvation"* (v. 16).
     b) **The Gospel Generates Saving Faith.** *"Every one that believes"* (v. 16).
  2) **The Simplicity of the Gospel.** *"For therein is the righteousness of God revealed from faith to faith; as it is written, The just shall live by faith"* (v. 17).
     a) **It is Revealed by Faith (v. 17).** *"Therein is the righteousness of God revealed from faith to faith"* (v. 17).
     b) **It is Received by Faith.** *"The just shall live by faith"* (v. 17).
C) **The Motivating Thrust.** From the *dominating theme* and *integrating thoughts* we learn what is the *motivating thrust*. It is twofold:
     a) **We Must Serve the Gospel.** Paul says he was *"separated unto the gospel of God"* as an apostle (v. 1), and he served the gospel with his spirit (v. 9).
     b) **We Must Share the Gospel.** So Paul declares, *"So, as much as in me is, I am ready to preach the gospel to you that are at Rome"* (v.15).

This is a simple demonstration of how to analyze and sermonize a passage of scripture. When we have *the subject, the structure,* and *the substance* of an expository sermon **written out in full**, it must become *incarnational* before we can deliver it. The manuscript must become the **message**. This *incarnational* experience can only come about as we pursue the following disciplines:

a) We Must Prayerfully Review the Sermon.
b) We Must Prayerfully Relate the Sermon.
c) We Must Prayerfully Rehearse the Sermon.
All this before we mount the pulpit!

In this process what is *instructional* becomes *incarnational*. This is what Phillips Brooks used to call "truth through personality." Like Mary of old, we must say from our hearts, "Be it unto me according to your word" (Luke 1:38). And if we really mean that prayer, the Word is *conceived* in us, and in due course we *deliver* Christ to the people. This is what preaching is all about.

So, **the GOLDEN HAMMER** helps to break down the *subject*, the *structure*, and when amplified and organized, the *sermon*, which God would have us preach from any given part of Holy Scripture. This applies to the diversified genre of scripture with the necessary adaptations to make clear to our listeners **what we are doing** with the text of God's Word. We must remember that the Bible contains narrative poetry, doctrine, prophecy, and other literary forms. But, in the final analysis, everything we preach must have a *dominating theme, integrating thoughts, and motivating thrust.* This is where **the GOLDEN HAMMER** proves its worth! For an example of developing a full sermon on a Scroggie *outline* see the next chapter!

2
A Look at Psalm 1

I remember Dr. Scroggie giving a brief chapel devotional on "The Man of God" from Psalm One, using the following points:

1) What he is negatively (v.1)
2) What he is positively (v.2)
3) What he is consequently (v.3)[2]

Later in my ministry, I expanded my own version with the expository sermon found on the next page!

---

2 See full treatment in book, A Guide To The Psalms, Kregel Publications, Grand Rapids, pp 48-50.

THE MAN OF GOD

Reading: Psalm 1

Introduction: This first Psalm is a fitting introduction to the sacred Psalter. Indeed, it constitutes a perfect summation of the whole book of Psalms, for it describes man as God intends him to be.

Like the Sermon on the Mount, this hymn begins with the word "blessed", and then goes on to show how blessedness and godliness are inseparably joined together.

The Psalmist then concludes with a striking contrast in which the ungodly man is portrayed both in his character and his condemnation. Let us, then, consider "The Man Of God."

Observe, first of all:

A. WHAT THE MAN OF GOD IS NEGATIVELY.

"Blessed is the man that walketh not in the counsel of the ungodly, nor standeth in the way of sinners, nor sitteth in the seat of the scornful" (v. 1).

We must remember that there is a negative side to godliness. There are some things which the man of God will not do. There is a divine nature within his personality, which is diametrically opposed to that which is godless, sinful, and scornful.

I. He is Opposed to Godless Thinking.

"Blessed is the man that walketh not in the counsel of the ungodly..." (v.1). His manner of life is not directed by the wisdom of this world, but rather by the wisdom which is from above. His philosophy of life is not sensual or earthly, but rather spiritual and divine. Instead of going to the world for his advice, he daily seeks his counsel from heaven. This is vitally important, for the Bible tells us that as a man *"...thinketh in his heart, so is he"*, (Prov. 23:7). As the familiar saying goes, "Sow a thought, reap a word; sow a word, reap an action; sow an action, reap a habit; sow a habit, reap a character; sow a character, reap a destiny."

II. He is Opposed to Lawless Living.

"...Nor standeth in the way of sinners..." (v.1). While godlessness may be defined as the ignorance of God, sinfulness is the

26

deliberate violation of the divine law. John declares in his epistle that *"...sin is the transgression of the law,"* or literally, lawlessness (1 Jn. 3:4).

Now the man of God believes in the absolute standard of God's revealed will for mankind. He will not accept the philosophy of the double standard or of relative values. How desperately we need this form of negativism in Christian circles today! It is so refreshing to meet anyone who stoutly opposes the general lawlessness of these times.

III. He is Opposed to Careless Speaking.

"...Nor sitteth in the seat of the scornful" (v.1). Those who begin to walk in the counsel of the ungodly usually end up sitting in the seat of the scornful. This is the chief seat in the kingdom of Satan. Those who occupy this position are filled with pride and contempt, and therefore speak with utter carelessness and scornfulness. May God preserve every Christian from ever reaching such a state of backsliding!

The retrogression described here is quite frightening:

Walking
    Standing
        Sitting
Counsel
    Way
        Seat
Ungodly
    Sinners
        Scornful

These are successive steps in a career of evil, and each category comes to a climax. There is a sense in which Peter, in his hour of backsliding, passed through the experience of *"walking in the counsel of the ungodly," "standing in the way of sinners,"* and *"sitting in the seat of the scornful";* for when he sat by the fireside and denied his Lord with oaths and curses, he had reached the place of utter defeat and spiritual declension. Thank God, he repented and returned to his former spiritual strength and effectiveness.

So we have seen that the man of God is distinguished by what he is negatively. In the next place, notice:

B. WHAT THE MAN OF GOD IS POSITIVELY.

"But his delight is in the law of the Lord; and in his law doth he meditate day and night" (v.2).

We saw just now that there is a negative side to godliness, and likewise there is a positive side.

The Psalmist shows us that the man of God, who lives positively, is known by:

I. His Appreciation of the Word of God.

"His delight is in the law of the Lord..." (v.2). Like David, in one of his later Psalms, he can say:

"The law of the Lord is perfect, converting the soul: the testimony of the Lord is sure, making wise the simple. The statutes of the Lord are right, rejoicing the heart: the commandment of the Lord is pure, enlightening the eyes. The judgments of the Lord are true and righteous altogether. More to be desired are they than 'honey and the honeycomb'" (Ps. 19:7-10).

The life of blessedness can never be separated from reading and studying the Bible. One of the greatest sins of this age is the neglect of God's Holy Word. This is why we have such weak and ineffective Christians in our churches. God make us like Thomas a Kempis, who was always saying,

"I have no rest, but in a nook with the Book." The New Testament exhortation is,

"Study to show thyself approved unto God, a workman that needeth not to be ashamed, rightly dividing the word of truth" (2 Tim. 2:15).

The man of God is also positively known by:

II. His Appropriation of the Word of God.

"And in his law doth he meditate day and night" (v.2). This was no chore to the Psalmist, for he said, *"Oh how love I thy law! it is my meditation all the day"* (Ps. 119:97).

It is one thing to appreciate the Bible for its literary excellence, its theological concepts, and its practical counsel, but quite another thing to appropriate its message and live out its doctrine in daily obedience.

The art of meditation involves appropriation; indeed, meditation is as needful to our spiritual health and strength as mastication is to the physical. Jeremiah knew something about this in his spiritual experience, for he testified, *"Thy words were found, and I did eat them; and thy word was unto me the joy and rejoicing of mine heart"* (Jer. 15:16).

One of the dangers in church life today is to be so objective in our view of the Bible that we fail to relate it to our daily living. Holiness is nothing less than the Holy Bible worked out in everyday experience.

God make us men and women who not only appreciate the Word of God, but appropriate it. Only thus shall we enter into the fullness of the blessing which God has revealed to us in the Holy Scriptures.

Once more, consider:

C. WHAT THE MAN OF GOD IS CONSEQUENTLY.

"And he shall be like a tree planted by the rivers of water, that bringeth forth his fruit in his season; his leaf also shall not wither; and whatsoever he doeth shall prosper" (v. 3).

When the circuit of Christian experience is closed, there flows a life of true blessedness. In exquisite language the characteristics of such a life are here enumerated for us. There is:

I. Constant Stability.

"He shall be like a tree planted..." (v. 3). Today, when there is so much inconstancy and unsteadiness, how wonderful to think of a life which is characterized by stability: *"a tree planted"*; therefore a life *"...grounded and settled, and...not moved away from the hope of the gospel..."* (Col. 1:23).

We can remember trees that were landmarks in our experience. From early childhood right through to manhood, the tree has remained immovable, majestic and beautiful; a shelter for all who sought its shade, and a refuge for those who hid among its branches and foliage. The Lord Jesus said, *"Every plant, which my heavenly Father hath not planted, shall be rooted up"* (Matt. 15:13).

But if a tree is planted by God, then we can depend upon

its stability. God makes us like strong trees planted by rivers of water!

II. Constant Sufficiency.

"He shall be like a tree planted by the rivers of water..." (v. 3).

Water is a symbol of the ministry of the Holy Spirit. The true believer, therefore, reaches down to this fountain of living water and draws upon the constant sufficiency of the divine life. There is no drought or dryness in such a life, but rather the freshness and fullness of the Holy Spirit.

III. Constant Fertility.

"Bringeth forth his fruit in his season..." (v. 3). Here is the picture of Christian fruitfulness. The Apostle Paul tells us that *"The fruit of the Spirit is love, joy, peace, long-suffering, gentleness, goodness, faith, meekness, temperance: against such there is no law"* (Gal. 5:22-23).

The Master declared, *"Herein is my Father glorified, that ye bear much fruit"* (John 15:8). How wonderful to bear the fruit of the Spirit in season—to produce love, when this quality is called for; joy, when there is need for joy; peace, when the demand is for peace; and so on. This is the ministry of the Spirit in us and through us as we "trust and obey."

IV. Constant Vitality.

"His leaf also shall not wither..." (v. 3).

The tree in Scripture is always the evidence of life. When God planted the Garden of Eden, it was full of trees (Gen. 2:8-17); when Ezekiel's river flowed out from the sanctuary, it produced trees along its banks with fruit for eating and leaves for healing (Ezek. 47:1-12). Again, what a picture this is of a Christian in whom the life of God is being constantly released!

There is a vital link between the root and the leaf. Dry roots soon bring dry rot into the leaves. People cannot see the roots of the Christian's character, but they can detect the leaf. It follows, therefore, that the hidden condition of the roots may be judged by the outward appearance of the leaf. If the outward life is fresh and green, then it is obvious that the inward life is pure and full. Withered leaves are a sign of a withered life. When our testimony for the Lord Jesus Christ loses its freshness and power, we may be sure that there is something wrong with the roots. It is certain that there is nothing wrong with the rivers of water, for they never run dry, neither do they become polluted. If, therefore, the tree is drawing from the rivers of living water, we can be confident of a perpetual display of evergreen foliage. It should be our constant prayer that *"The beauty of the Lord our God* [might] *be upon us"* (Ps. 90:17).

V. Constant Prosperity.

"Whatsoever he doeth shall prosper" (v.3).

There is another rendering which reads, *"And whatsoever he doeth shall come to maturity."* It is God's design for our lives that we should ever be moving on to maturity, growing up into Christ until we arrive *"unto the measure of the stature of the fullness of Christ"* (Eph. 4:13); or to put it in other words, until we are *"conformed to the image of God's Son"* (Rom. 8:29).

There is also the thought here of spiritual success– *"whatsoever he doeth shall prosper"* (v.3). How wonderful it is to have such spiritual success guaranteed in all we seek to say and do in the work of God.

This, then, is the overflow and outflow of a life that is negatively and positively adjusted to the will of God. This is surely true blessedness in the highest sense.

What a contrast this is to the ungodly life! The Psalmist tells us that they *"...are like the chaff which the wind driveth away. Therefore the ungodly shall not stand in the judgment, nor sinners in the congregation of the righteous. For the Lord knoweth the way of the righteous: but the way of the ungodly shall perish"* (vv. 4-6).

Notice that the ungodly are not trees, but chaff. The one defies the storm while the other is driven before it. To stand *"in the way of sinners"* means not to stand in the day of judgment; so *"the way of the ungodly"* must perish, for it is the way of godless thinking, lawless living, and careless speaking. *"There is a way which seemeth right unto a man; but the end thereof are the ways of death"* (Prov. 14:12).

God deliver us from anything less than the blessedness which He has purposed for men and women after His own heart!

The Problem of Plagiarism

Before opening up the treasure trove of Dr. Graham Scroggie's personally produced and proclaimed Biblical outlines (never before published), a word about the problem of plagiarism is in order.

Plagiarism is defined as "literary theft," "presenting a new or an original product without crediting the source." This breech of integrity is committed all the time–even among preachers! It is wrong, and therefore, displeasing to God.

What, then, shall we do with the materials that are offered in this book? The answer is simple.

Right up front, we must acknowledge with gratefulness that we are using or quoting sermon helps from the words of (in this case) Dr. Graham Scroggie. Now, of course, this cannot be done endlessly without affecting our congregations. They wonder whether we do anything creative or original in our studies! On the other hand, no scholar of any repute writes commentaries, sermons, or theology without liberal use of footnotes! It reveals the measure of his research. Indeed, even some commentaries contain as many footnotes and references on one page as to equal the substance of what he has written in the text!

The answer to all this is a balanced approach with literary honesty. There is no reason in the world why a preacher cannot adopt and adapt an outline or a paraphrased quotation without committing plagiarism. If it is a strict quote or use of an outline – state the fact without laboring the point: i.e., "I am indebted to (Dr.'s name) for this insightful thought, quote, or outline."

On the other hand, there is nothing humanly original in the ultimate sense; and there is plenty of encouragement from the Word of God to support this. Exhorting young Timothy to fulfill the ministry, Paul says, *"The things that you have heard from me* *among many witnesses, commit **these** to faithful men who will be able to teach others also"* (2 Tim. 2:2). And that principle has governed all of Christian tradition.

I thank God for men in the ministry who have shared with their congregations what I had just shared with them, and then wrote to tell me! Indeed, I would be just as happy if they did not tell me!

I enjoy the outlines and studies from the heart and pen of Dr. Graham Scroggie; and I trust that you will also!

SFO (Stephen Olford)

3
Outlines
Scroggie on Revival

REVIVAL NO. 1
"Wilt thou not revive us again?" (Ps. 85:6).

I. The Need for a true and widespread revival.
II.The Nature of a true and widespread revival.

I. THE NEED FOR A TRUE REVIVAL
1. That the church may realize her union with Christ.
2. That the Gospel may be carried to the ends of the earth.
3. That the time may be hastened when Israel will be restored and the Gentiles blessed.
4. That the way may be prepared for the establishment of the Kingdom.

II.THE NATURE OF A TRUE REVIVAL
1. Conviction and confession of Sin.
2. Graciousness and full deliverance from Bondage.
3. New sense of the Power of the Cross.
4. New experience of the glow of Divine Life.
5. Practical recognition of the Lordship of Christ.
6. Fresh love for and dependence on the Holy Spirit.
7. Divine zeal for the salvation of Men.

Dr. Olford's comments are in side bars throughout the outlines! Marked by the initials: SFO.

SFO Notes

This is a good example of a Topical Sermon. No doubt Scroggie intended it as an introduction to the series on Revival that follows. Otherwise, he rarely preached non-expository sermons.

The text Psalm 85:6 is a good one for a revival sermon. Here is a suggested outline: Have an appropriate introduction to the Psalm that forecasts the possibility of a coming national revival–we have three reasons why God sends revival:

I. **Revival Restrains the Righteous Anger of God** (vv. 4-7)
    It is clear from these verses that God must visit His righteous anger against **unrepentant people**.
    Note: the three words used to describe this condition: *"the **iniquity** of your people"* (v.2); *"all their sin"* (v.2); *"let them not turn back to **folly**"* (v.8).

II. **Revival Restores the Conscious Awareness of God** (v.6)
     Note: The smiling of His face (v.6); The showing of His grace (v.7); The sounding of His voice (v.8).

III. **Revival Reveals the Gracious Activity of God**
     Note: Saving activity (v.9); Sanctifying activity in the rest of the Psalms (vs. 10-13).

REVIVAL NO. 2

"I will pour out my Spirit upon all flesh" (Joel 2:28).

Consider: The Promise of the Spirit
The Power of the Spirit
The Place of the Spirit

THE PROMISE OF THE SPIRIT FOR QUICKENING AND REVIVAL
(Isa. 32:15. Ezek. 39:29. Joel 2:28,32. Zech. 12:10).

I. THE NATURE OF THIS BLESSING ... A MIGHTY OUTPOURING

1. The Origin of it—Heavenly.
"Poured out...from on high" (Isa. 32:15).
It does not arise from within, but descends from above.

2. The Measure of it—Abundant.
"Poured out."
Not droppings, but a deluge.

3. The Action of it—Continuous.
"Poured out."
Heb: imperfect tense.

II. THE CONSEQUENCES OF THIS BLESSING–TENFOLD

1. Deliverance from Bondage.
a. The sinner will be delivered from the tyranny of Satan
(Col. 1:13; Acts 26:18).
b. The believer will be delivered from the bondage of Sin.
(2 Cor. 3:17).
c. Israel, ultimately will be delivered from Captivity.
(Ezek. 39:27-29; Joel 2:32).

38

2.Lips unsealed for Testimony. (Joel 2:28; Acts 2:2; 4:31).

3.Eyes purged for vision.
   (Joel 2:28; 1 Cor. 12:9-10)

4.A gracious Spirit.
   (Zech. 12:10).

5.Power in Prayer.
   (Zech. 12:10; Eph. 6:18).

6.Wonder working among Men.
   (Joel 2:30).

7.Fruitfulness instead of Barrenness.
   (Isa. 32:15).

8.Righteousness instead of Iniquity.
   (Isa. 32:16).

9.Security and rest in danger and Upheaval.
   (Isa. 32:18,19).

REVIVAL NO. 3
Revival and the Word

I. **KNOWLEDGE OF THE WORD** (Isa. 34:16).
    1. The Bible is a revelation from God to man. (Heb. 1:1-2).
    2. To know the nature of that revelation, man must study the Bible.
    3. Where there is ignorance of the Word, revival gives the devil unique opportunities.

II. **FAITH IN THE WORD** (Isa. 7:9).
    1. We must believe the Bible to be the Word of God (1 Thess. 2:13).
    2. We must believe the Bible to be the Power of God (Rom. 1:18).
    3. Where there is no faith, there can be no Revival (Matt. 13:58).

III. **OBEDIENCE TO THE WORD** (Josh. 1:7-8).
    1. The Bible, being what it is, demands one's obedience.
    2. Obedience is everywhere made a condition of blessing. (Deut. 11:27. Gen. 22:18. Exod. 19:5. Job. 36:11).
    3. Disobedience is the most effective hindrance to Revival.

IV. **VICTORY THROUGH THE WORD** (Eph. 6:17; Matt. 4:1-11).
    1. The Bible is the weapon of warfare with Evil.
    2. Every true movement of the Spirit necessitates conflict with Evil.
    3. Victory is revival and victory is through the Word.

SFO Notes

This is a good outline on Revival and the Word of God; but the individual sub-headings require appropriate Scripture support. Add these before developing the full sermon.

REVIVAL NO. 4
The Need and Conditions of Revival
(Mal. 3:7-12)

I. THE COMPLAINT OF JEHOVAH AGAINST HIS PEOPLE. (7-9).
II.THE COVENANT OF JEHOVAH WITH HIS PEOPLE. (10-12).

I. THE COMPLAINT OF JEHOVAH AGAINST HIS PEOPLE 7-9.
    1. The Charge Preferred. (7).
    2. The Charge Enforced. (8,9).

1.THE CHARGE PREFERRED. 7.
"From the days of your fathers ye have turned aside from mine ordinances, and have not kept them."

I. THE ACCUSATION.
    A. The Word of God is the revelation of spiritual character regarding truth and the test of loyalty or disobedience to God. *"Mine ordinances"*.
        "If ye love me, keep my commandments" (John 14:15).
    B. Departure from the Word is disobedience.
        (Pos:) *"turned aside,"* (Neg:) *"have not kept."*
    C. The prevalence of continuousness of this sin among God's people.
        "From the days of your fathers."

II. THE APPEAL RETURN.
"Return unto me, and I will return unto you."
    A. Disobedience puts distance between the Soul and God.
        Implied by the call to *"Return"*.
    B. The wanderer is called upon to retrace his steps.
        "Return unto Me." cf: Abram. Peter.
    C. The assurance is given of reinstatement unto the Divine Favor.
        "I will return unto you." (cf: Hosea 14).

III. **THE ANSWER. WHEREIN.** cf: *"wherein"* 7 times.
The worst feature of their condition was their INSENSI-
BILITY of need. Being far from God they thought they
were near. Sick of soul, they thought they were well. But
their demand of proof of the charge, the Lord accepts.

2. THE CHARGE ENFORCED (8,9).

I. THE NATURE (EXPRESSION) OF THEIR SIN.
Defraudment of God.
*"Will a man rob God? Yet ye have robbed Me. Wherein? In tithes
and offerings."*
"Tithes and offerings" were for the maintenance of the Priests
and Levites who waited upon "the Divine Service." As that
Service was God's, to starve them was to rob Him.
It is robbery of God to withhold from Him aught that belongs to Him. We ourselves and all we have belong to Him,
so that if we withhold anything, we are robbing Him.
Multitudes of Christians are as insensible that they are robbing God, as were these Israelites. Every unsurrendered
soul is a robbery of God. It is essential to a true life to recog-
nize God's Proprietorship of all, and our own stewardship.
(Cf: 1 Chron. 29:14).

II. THE EXTENT OF THEIR SIN. "This whole nation".
Two things to observe:

A. That this sinful state and attitude was general. Is it less
general today?

B. That, on this account, God does not call them His peo-
ple, but, "this nation", a word employed generally of the
Gentiles: cf: 1:11.
They had ceased to be better than the heathen, and there-
fore were not worthy of a better name. (Not, *Ha-am*, but,
Ha-goi) cf: Israel, Jacob: Peter, Simon.
The backsliding of the Church today. There are always
loyal souls in it, as there were in Israel of old, but being

part of the whole, we must accept a measure of responsibility for the prevailing condition . Thus Daniel confessed Israel's sin as his own.

III. THE EFFECT OF THEIR SIN.
"Ye are cursed with the curse" (Cf: 2:2. Deut. 28). The curse referred to is a withholding of the harvests, and a corrupting of the fruits (Mal. 2:3).
The blessings and curses under the old dispensation were largely temporal (material): but in this dispensation, chiefly spiritual.
The evidence of a sinful state in any child of God is spiritual sterility, stagnation: life, but no growth; root, but little fruit. Spiritual enrichment cannot be present in the soul that is robbing God. We cannot enrich ourselves by robbing God.

II. THE COVENANT OF JEHOVAH WITH HIS PEOPLE (10-12).
1. The Conditions of Blessing. (10a).
2. The Consequences of Obedience. (10b-12).

1. THE CONDITIONS OF BLESSING. (10a).

I. PROMISE IS CONDITIONED UPON PRECEPT.
"Do what I command, and I will bless you".
Some of the Divine Promises are unconditional, and it is not in the power of man to prevent the fulfillment of these. Ex. Abrahamic Covenant. (Gen. 12).
But the majority of the Promises are conditioned. Ex:
(John 15:7) — *"If ye abide in Me...ye shall ask...shall be done"*.
(John 15:14) — Friendship conditioned on obedience.
(Jas. 1:5) — *"If any lack wisdom let him ask"* etc.
(Matt. 6:33) — *"Seek ye first the Kingdom of God and His righteousness, and all these things shall be added unto you."*
(Mal. 3:10) — *"Bring all the tithes...and I will"* etc.

When God conditions a Promise or a Precept, it is fooling with Him to ask for the fulfillment of the Promise while the Precept is disregarded. (Illus. How that is done with this v. 7).

III. GETTING IS CONDITIONED UPON GIVING.
"You bring in, and I'll pour out."

The law of the Spiritual life is, Get, Give, Keep.
If we Get, it is that we might Give, and only by Giving can we Keep what we Get.
(2 Cor. 9:6-8. cf: Prov. 3:9,10 with Luke 12:16-21).
(2 Cor. 8:2,3,12. Prov. 11:24,25. Matt. 10:8).

If we Get and fail to Give, we shall lose, and our Getting will be stopped. True of things Material (temporal) and Spiritual alike.

A. Thousands are losing inestimably in Material things, because they are not giving of their substance to God. The doctrine of Christian giving has almost passed out of out thinking: (and Concerts, Bazaars, and Entertainment have taken its place). (How is it that almost every Missionary Society is in debt today?)

B. And how incalculable is the loss of those who fail to give of the Grace which they receive! It is not Prosperity that is productive of Liberality, but the latter which is productive of the former. (Cf: 2 Chron: 31:10. 1Kgs. 17:13. 2 Cor. 8:2,3). Your present depression may be due to past unfaithfulness.

IV. FULL SALVATION IS CONDITIONED UPON FULL SURRENDER.
"Bring the whole tithe in ... such a blessing, there will not be room enough to receive it".
It is the whole-hearted who come in for the Super-abundance. "They who trust Him wholly, find Him wholly true." He gives all to those who yield all to Him. (cf: Caleb).

2. THE CONSEQUENCES OF OBEDIENCE. (10b-12).

I. SPIRITUAL PLATITUDE. 10b. ABUNDANCE. FULLNESS.

A. The Source of the blessing: *"I will"* –God Himself.
B. The Nature of the blessing: *"The windows of heaven"* (cf: Gen. 7:11).
"Blessed with all spiritual blessings in heavenly places" (Eph. 1:3).
The immediate reference in Malachi is to fertilization of the ground (cf: verse 11), but our portion is Spiritual.
C. The Measure of the blessing: *"Poured out: no room to receive."* (Cf: Gen. 7:11. Flooding blessing).

II. DIVINE PROTECTION. (11).

"I will rebuke the devourer."
The reference is to the locust, no doubt. (cf: Mal. 2:3). Not only does God give Fertility for Sterility, but He protects the fruit from the enemy, and brings it to maturity. *"Neither shall your vine cast her fruit before the time in the field."*

III. WIDE PROSPERITY. (12). ACKNOWLEDGMENT.

"All nations shall call you blessed, for ye shall be a delightsome land."
This is yet to be fulfilled concerning Israel. For it is when they shall turn to the Lord. It is a great thing when even the world calls them *"blessed"* who are Christ's: but they will do so, only as we wholly follow the Lord.
There are set before us two Pictures, which are also Parables:--
One of Sterility: Jeremiah 14:1-6.
One of Fertility: Isaiah 55:12, 13; 35:7-10.
Which of these is true of us, depends wholly on our attitude towards the Will of God.

REVIVAL NO. 5
Habakkuk 3:2

"O LORD, revive thy work in the midst of the years,
in the midst of the years make known;
in wrath remember mercy."

1. THE MEANING OF REVIVAL.

Quickening the dead. Renewal of the living. The gracious work of the Spirit of God upon the hearts of men.

2. THE NEED OF REVIVAL.

I. THE STATE OF THE WORLD (1942)

World wide war.

II. THE STATE OF THE CHURCHES.

A. Scepticism. Doctrine lost its power to convict and convince.
B. Formalism. Ritual becomes formal and lifeless.

III. THE PROSPECT OF REVIVAL.

"Wilt Thou not revive us again, that Thy people may rejoice in Thee?" (Ps. 85:6).

1. Revivals are subject to the common law of Progress.
"Not by a steady outward movement like the march of an army, but by an oscillating movement, like that of an incoming tide".
Intellectual, Scientific, material and commercial progress is made in this way. Waves rush up, and then recede, only to gather strength for another rush.
So it is with spiritual revival. It is worked by rush and recoil. cf: The Welsh Revival. Observable also is the experience of the individual. Exultation and depression. But the recoil is a preparation for another rush.

2. Conditions which usually precede revival.
A. Period of national development, of social or political change.

B. Dullness and deadness in the Church, cf: Sardis and Laodicea.

C. Dissatisfaction and longing in many hearts (Rev. 3:4). Gatherings for prayer.

D. Appearance of a Prophet–Leader, cf: Francis. Luther. Wesley.

IV. EVIDENCES OF REVIVAL

1. A deep sense of sin.
2. Confession.
3. Recovery of Calvary.
4. Out-rush of joy. Soul.

V. THE COST OF REVIVAL.

Always costly—involving renunciation, dedication, willingness to suffer, readiness to accept new adjustments and adaptations. The alternative today (1942) is ghastly. Nothing less than the precipice of unbelievable ruin for this world.

The conditions which have preceded other revivals are practically all present now: national transition, want of life, power, widespread dissatisfaction and longing. It may be that the hope and expectation of many is that a new spiritual dawn is about to break upon us.

SFO Notes

Read through the prophecy of Habakkuk and substantiate the main headings with relevant verses or paragraphs that relate to Chapter 3 and verse 2.

REVIVAL NO. 6
"Gather out the stones" (Isa. 62:10).

CONTEXT. CH. 62. INTERPRETATION. APPLICATION.

1. A GREAT OPPORTUNITY.
"Go through the gates"(cf: Rev. 3:8).

(Cf: 1Cor. 16:9). Present day opportunity. These are the gates of Babylon, and so it is a call to pass through into freedom. Backsliding is Bondage.

2. A SOLEMN RESPONSIBILITY.
"Prepare the way."

I. By casting up a highway.
i.e. Ways and means used to reach the people and bring them to Christ.

II. By gathering out the Stones.
i.e. The hindrances in personal and church life.

A. **Stones to be gathered out:**
Unfruitfulness, dishonesty, uncleanness, malice, bitterness, evil speaking, pride, indifference, unbelief, selfishness, cowardice, fear, criticism, opposition.

3. AN INESTIMABLE PRIVILEGE.
"Lift up a standard." Around which the gathering host may rally. (v. 12). The Cross of Christ.

4. HINDRANCES MUST BE REMOVED.
A. **Debts must be paid.**
B. **Restitution must be made.**
C. **Evil-speaking must cease.**

48

D. Sinful habits must be broken.
E. Indifference must end.
F. Unbelief must give way.
G. Wrong doing must be confessed.
H. Pride must be brought low.
I. Fear must be overcome.
J. Bitterness must be banished.
K. Indolence must be cast aside.
L. Malice must perish.

SFO Notes

Study each of these hindrances and find an appropriate verse (consistent with context) to fit each one.

4
Outlines on the
Churches in Revelation

OUTLINE NO. 7
Christ and the Churches
Rev. 1:9-20.

The Setting (9-12)
The Subject Of the vision (13-16)
The Sequence (17-20).

I. THE SETTING OF THE VISION. (9-12).
"I saw seven golden lampstands." A sevenfold symbolism of:

1. THE FUNCTION OF THE CHURCHES
Lamps are for light. Knowledge and truth.

2. THE DEPENDENCE OF THE CHURCHES
Lamp light is borrowed. Sunlight.

3. THE TIME OF THE CHURCHES
Lamps are for the night.

4. THE DIVERSITY OF THE CHURCHES
Lamps, not one but many.

5. THE UNITY OF THE CHURCHES
Light gives unity to all the lamps.

6. THE CHARACTER OF THE CHURCHES
"Golden" lampstands. Purity. Preciousness.

7. THE COMPLETENESS OF THE CHURCHES
"Seven": This number in *"Revelation."*
The corporate and complete testimony for Christ on earth during His absence from it.

II. THE SUBJECT OF THE VISION. (13-16).
"In the midst...the Son of Man."

Mystical: not, "in the middle" –Geometrical.

"In the midst of the:
A. Doctors. (Luke 2:46)	Learning.
B. Prayer-meeting. (Matt. 18:20).	Devotion.
C. Fearing Disciples. (John 20:19,26).	Distress. Perplexity.
D. Crosses. (John 19:18)	Suffering.
E. Churches. (Rev. 1:13).	Christianity.
G. Throne. (Rev. 7:17).	Universal Kingdom

Description of the Son of Man in His Relation to the Churches.

1. HIS OFFICIAL DIGNITY—HIS BODY.
"Clothed with a garment down to the foot."
   a. As Priest–to Mediate.
   b. As King –to Rule.
   c. As Judge -to Sentence.

2. HIS INTENSE AFFECTION—HIS BREASTS.
"Girt about the breasts with a golden girdle."
   a. Breasts –seat of emotion, love.
   b. Girt –all affection knit up into a compact unity.
   c. Golden -purity and preciousness.

3. HIS PERFECT HOLINESS—HIS HEAD
"His head and his hairs were white like wool, as white as snow."
   a. Not the Symbol of old age, but
   b. The Transfiguration in light of His glorious Person
   c. His essential and perfect Holiness

4. HIS CONSUMING KNOWLEDGE—HIS EYES.
"His eyes were as a flame of fire."
   a. EYES– the symbol of Knowledge.
   b. FIRE –the symbol of the Divine Anger.

c. HIS–knowledge of, and attitude towards evil among His People.

5. HIS RIGHTEOUS Judgment— HIS FEET.
"His feet like unto fine brass, as if they burned in a furnace."
   a. BRASS–the symbol of Judgment.
   b. THE STRENGTH OF IT–"brass."
   c. THE FIERCENESS OF IT–"burnished brass."

6. HIS ABSOLUTE AUTHORITY—HIS VOICE
"His voice as the sound of many waters."
   a. ONE VOICE–many waters.
   b. ALL POSSIBLE NOTES–mercy, anger, comfort, rebuke, love.
   c. THE MANY MESSAGES OF THE PAST–in the one revelation of the Present.

7. HIS SOVEREIGN ADMINISTRATION—HIS RIGHT HAND.
"In His right hand Seven Stars."
   a. THE STARS–ministers called and ordained of God.
   b. SEVEN -throughout the Christian dispensation.
   c. IN RIGHT HAND - Representation, Control, Security.

8. HIS ALL-SEARCHING TRUTH—HIS MOUTH.
"Out of His mouth went a sharp two-edged sword."
   a. SWORD-that which pierces and penetrates.
   b. MOUTH-SWORD- His Word of Truth. (Heb. 4:12. Isa. 49:2).
   c. TWO-EDGED–O.T. & N.T. (Tertullian); Law & Grace.

9. HIS TRANSCENDENT GLORY—HIS COUNTENANCE.
"His countenance was as the sun shineth in his strength."
   a. COUNTENANCE–expressive of character.
   b. AS THE SUN- brightness of glory.
   c. IN HIS STRENGTH-at midday, no veil or cloud.

III. THE SEQUENCE OF THE VISION. (17-20).
"I fell at His feet as dead."
"Fear not."

1. **HIS ETERNAL BEING.**
   "I am the First and the Last."

   a. THE ETERNITY OF CHRIST—*"I am the First."*
   b. THE DEITY OF CHRIST
   c. THE FINALITY OF CHRIST
   d. THE VICTORY OF CHRIST— "I am the Last."

2. **HIS INDISSOLUBLE LIFE.**
   "And the Living One."
   a. CHRIST AND THE FULLNESS OF LIFE.
   b. CHRIST THE FOUNTAIN OF LIFE.

3. **HIS ATONING SACRIFICE.**
   "And I became dead."
   a. THE FACT OF CHRIST'S DEATH.
   b. THE VOLUNTARINESS OF CHRIST'S DEATH.

4. **HIS GLORIOUS VICTORY.**
   "And, behold, I am alive for evermore."
   a. HIS RESURRECTION THE COMPLETION OF HIS ATONING WORK.
   b. HIS RESURRECTION LIFE AND POWER

5. **HIS SOVEREIGN LORDSHIP.**
   "And I have the keys of Death and Hades."
   a. HE HAS THE KEY OF DEATH—THE POWER.
   b. HE HAS THE KEY OF HADES—THE PLACE.

SFO Notes

Fill in actual verse numbers to main points before writing our sermon in full.

A Look at Two Letters to the churches: Ephesus, Sardis

OUTLINE NO. 8
The Letter to Ephesus
(Rev. 2:1-7).

All seven letters are constructed on the same model: an Address, and seven parts. Two are without Praise, two are without Blame, and three have both Praise and Blame.

I. THE ADDRESS. (1a)
  A. THE AUTHOR OF THE LETTER: THE GLORIFIED LORD
  B. THE WRITER OF THE LETTER: THE APOSTLE JOHN
  C. THE DESTINATION OF THE LETTER EPHESUS

    The destination is to: 1. The Angel–the presiding Elder
                                   2. The Church-through the Angel
                                   3. The City–at Ephesus

II. THE LETTER. (1b-7)
  A. A WORD OF RELATION. (1b).

    1. SOME ATTRIBUTE OR FUNCTION OF CHRIST, IS TAKEN FROM THE PREVIOUS DESCRIPTION (1:13-18) AND APPLIED TO THE CHURCH IN VIEW OF ITS STATE.

    2. THE STATE ADDRESSED
Spiritual declension: Religious conventionalism.

    3. THE LORD REVEALED.
(1:16) The Source and Sustainer of Light "Stars"
The Observer and Judge of the Lightbearers "Lampstand"

  B. A WORD OF ESTIMATE. (2,3,6)
    1. THEIR SERVICE IS COMMENDED (2a)
      a. It is Actual–*"works"*
      b. It is Costly–*"toil"*
      c. It is Persistent –*"patience"*

2. THEIR DISCIPLINE IS COMMENDED. (2b, 6)
   A. As to Conduct–*"canst not bear evil men"*
   B. As to Creed– *"didst try ... and find false"*

3. THEIR ENDURANCE IS COMMENDED (3).
   A. It was Persistent – *"patience"*
   B. It was Loyal – *"hast borne for My Name's sake"*
   C. It was Vigorous – *"hast not grown weary"*

III. A WORD OF REBUKE (4) *"But"*
   ### 1. THE CHARGE PREFERRED.
   A charge, not of commission, but of omission: Loss of First Love.
   (1 Thess. 1:3). Work of Faith: Labor of Love: Patience of Hope.
   ### 2. THE OCCASION POINTED TO— *"Thou didst leave"*
   ### 3. THE EFFECT PRODUCED— *"I have this against thee."*
   (Possible to hate what Christ hates, without loving what He loves).

IV. A WORD OF COUNSEL (5a)
   ### 1. A CALL TO RECOLLECTION—Remember Think
   ### 2. A CALL TO REPENTANCE—Repent Feel
   ### 3. A CALL TO RENEWAL—Return Act

5. A WORD OF WARNING.
   ### 1. THE THREAT Removal of lampstand.
   ### 2. THE POWER I will come and do it.
   ### 3. THE FULFILLMENT Condition of Ephesus today.

6. A WORD OF COMMAND (7)
   ### 1. THE APPLICATION OF THE LETTERS IS UNIVERSAL *"to the churches"*
   ### 2. THE APPEAL OF THE LETTER IS INDIVIDUAL *"he...him"*
   ### 3. THE AUTHORITY OF THE LETTER IS FINAL *"the Spirit saith"*

7. A WORD OF PROMISE (7)
   ### 1. TO WHOM THE PROMISE IS MADE *"the Overcomer"*
   ### 2. BY WHOM THE PROMISE IS MADE *"I will give"*
   ### 3. THE PROMISE THAT IS MADE *"give to eat of Tree of Life"*
   It corresponds to the faithfulness exhibited.

OUTLINE NO. 9
The Sardian Letter
(Rev. 3:1-6)

I. THE CONNECTION:
   1. THE STATE OF THE CHURCH.
      A. Spiritual torpor of death.
      B. Effete and moribund faith.

   2. THE SUITABILITY OF THE ADDRESS.
      A. Source of spiritual fullness and power.
      B. Author of spiritual ministry for communication and maintenance.

II. THE CENSURE
   1. FAME OF THE CHURCH'S ACTIVITY—*"a name to live"*
   2. FUTILITY OF THE CHURCH'S ACTIVITY—*"thou art dead"*
   3. FAULT OF THE CHURCH'S ACTIVITY—*"no work fulfilled before God"*

III. THE COUNSEL: A SUMMON TO
   1. RECOVERY—Present participle: *"Become watching"*
   2. REMEMBRANCE—Present imperative: *"Continue to remember"*
   3. REPENTANCE—Aorist: *"Repent once and for all"*

IV. THE CAUTION: THREAT OF DIVINE VISITATION
   1. IT IS ANNOUNCED— *"I will come upon thee"*
   2. IT IS CONDITIONED— *"if"*
   3. IT IS DESCRIBED—*"As a thief"*

V. THE COMMENDATION
   1. THE LORD'S RECOGNITION OF THESE—*"a few in Sardis"*
   2. THE LORD'S RECOMMENDATION OF THEM—*"have not defiled"*
   3. THE LORD'S REWARD TO THEM—*"shall walk with Me"*

VI. THE CALL
   1. TO PERFECT HOLINESS— *"arrayed in white"*
   2. TO ETERNAL FELLOWSHIP—*"ever in the book of life"*
   3. TO CELESTIAL HONOR—*"I will confess"*

VII. THE COMMAND—*"Hear"*

SFO Notes

This is a magnificent treatment of the Sardian letter. Read it carefully and add verse numbers to each of the main and supporting points (even for sub-headings)–and write out the sermon in full.

General Outlines
in Revelation

OUTLINE NO. 10
Christ the Inclusive and Eternal Fact
(Rev. 22:13)

I. OF MATERIAL CREATION, HE IS THE BEGINNING OF THE END

A. THE ORIGINATOR OF ALL
"For by him were all things created, that are in heaven, and that are in earth, visible and invisible, whether they be thrones, or dominions, or principalities, or powers; all things were created by him, and for him." (Col. 1:16).

B. THE MAINTAINER OF ALL
"By Him all things subsist" (Col. 1:17).

C. THE POSSESSOR OF ALL
"the firstborn [Heir] *of every creature"* (Col. 1:15).

II. OF WRITTEN REVELATION, HE IS THE ALPHA AND THE OMEGA
The first and last letters of the Greek alphabet; suggesting literature-Scripture.

A. IN THE OLD TESTAMENT, WE HAVE PROPHETIC ANTICIPATION OF CHRIST
a. His Human Pedigree
b. His Redemptive Programme
c. His Divine Person

B. IN THE GOSPELS, WE HAVE PERSONAL MANIFESTATION OF CHRIST
a. As Life—Quickening
b. As Light—Illuminating
c. As Love—Compelling

C. IN THE ACTS TO REVELATION, WE HAVE APOSTOLIC INTER-PRETATION OF CHRIST

    a. In Acts—The Prophet of Yesterday
    b. In Epistles—The Priest of Today
    c. In Revelation—The King of Tomorrow

III. OF HUMAN HISTORY, HE IS THE FIRST AND THE LAST

A. ALL ITS COMMENCEMENTS WERE BY HIS WILL

B. ALL ITS PROCESSES ARE IN HIS WISDOM

C. ALL ITS ISSUES SHALL BE UNDER HIS POWER

Beginning and End, Alpha and Omega, First and Last.
Christ is the inclusive and Eternal Fact, and significance is given to life only as it is related to Him. Where do you stand in relation to Christ?

SFO Notes

Follow instructions suggested under outlines 8 & 9.

OUTLINE NO. 11
Peril of Loss

"Behold, I come quickly: hold that fast which thou hast, that no man take thy crown" (Rev. 3:11).

Only two of the seven churches receive no rebuke–Smyrna and Philadelphia, but even the exemplary need to be warned. Observe four things in our text:

I. A BLESSING TO BE COVETED—A CROWN

1. *"CROWN"*

Tells of a consummation. Here, not a crown of dominion, but of victory.

2. *"CROWNS"*

Four: of Life, Glory, Righteousness, Rejoicing.
A. First Two consisting of Life and Glory.
B. Second Two rewards of Character and Service.

3. *"THY CROWN"*

Ours only in possibility, not in actuality, for the end is not yet. Ours if we win it–and we may. A recompense at the end if the end merits it.
Something for each of us.

II. A DANGER TO BE FEARED—THE LOSS OF OUR CROWN

1. DISTINCTION BETWEEN GIFT, WAGES, REWARD
A. A Gift is Bestowed—*"the free gift of God"*–etc.
B. A Wage is Earned— *"the wages of sin"* –etc.
C. A Reward is Won

2. THE POSSIBLE MAY NEVER BECOME ACTUAL
We may lose our crown by never receiving it.
A. The race may be lost in the last lap.
B. Our boat may be wrecked near the shore.

C. The campaign may be lost in the last battle.
D. The end may rob the beginning.

Illustration: SAMSON, SAUL, DAVID.
Paul feared that at last he might be a *"castaway."*

3. HOW POSSESSION MAY BE FRUSTRATED.
A. By carelessness
B. By compromise
C. By capitulation
Esau sold his birthright. Moses failed to cross the Jordan.

III. A COMMAND TO BE OBEYED.
"Hold fast that which thou hast."

1. WHAT THE CHRISTIAN HAS–TO *"HOLD FAST."*
A. Spiritual attainments and achievements, Phil. 3:16
B. Enrichment of Knowledge
C. Fruit of Service
D. Privilege of Association
E. Greatness of Opportunity

2. WAYS IN WHICH TO *"HOLD FAST."* BY
A. A proper use of the Word of God.
B. Diligence in Prayer.
C. Carefully selected reading.
D. A choice of true friendships.
E. Definite service for Christ.

3. THE DUTY TO *"HOLD FAST."* IT IS A DUTY
A. To God
B. To ourselves
C. To others
No one can rob us of our crown but ourselves.

4. A REASON TO BE REGARDED.
"Behold, I come quickly."

A. The influence of the Future on the Present
B. The prospect of Accountability
C. The dimensions of Time and Eternity

OUTLINE NO. 12
THE LAST Judgment
REV. 20:11-15.

I. THE FINALITY OF IT

1. IT WILL BE RIGHTEOUS
"a great white throne"—Fairness

2. IT WILL BE COMPLETE
"a white throne"—Holiness

3. IT WILL BE TERRIBLE
God the Judge—Sovereignty

II. THE SUBJECTS OF IT.

1. ALL SINNERS.
"the dead"—Universality

2. EVERYONE—Particularity

3. ACCORDING TO WORKS—Touchstone

III. THE PROCEDURE OF IT

1. THE DEAD ARE RESURRECTED
Sea-death-hades yield up

2. THE DEAD ARE ASSEMBLED
"standing before the throne"

3. THE DEAD ARE JUDGED FROM RECORDS
"the books" "the book of life"

IV. THE ISSUES OF IT.

1. EXCLUSION FROM GOD 15a *"not in the book of life"*

2. THE LAKE OF FIRE (15b)

3. ETERNAL DEATH (14b) *"the second"*

OUTLINE NO. 13
THE ETERNAL STATE

"Behold, I make all things new" (Rev. 21:5).

The setting of this passage is Revelation 21:1–22:5, in the *"Unveiling."*
1. THE CHRISTIAN AGE
2. THE TRIBULATION
3. THE MILLENNIAL REIGN
4. THE ETERNAL STATE

I. IN THIS LAST, ALL THINGS ARE TO BE NEW AND PERMANENT.
1. ALL THINGS EARTHLY WILL BE NEW.
"I saw a new earth" (v. 1).

2. ALL THINGS HEAVENLY WILL BE NEW.
"I saw a new heaven" (v. 1).

3. THE RELATION BETWEEN THE EARTHLY AND THE HEAVENLY WILL BE NEW.
"I saw the New Jerusalem coming down from God out of heaven:-and I heard a voice saying, 'The Tabernacle of God is with men" (vv. 2-3).

II. ALL THINGS EARTHLY WILL BE NEW
THE EARTH ITSELF, AS A SPHERE OF ABODE, WILL BE NEW.

1. IT IS NEVER TO BECOME EXTINCT.
The common notion is that it is to entirely pass away, cf. Cato, "The wreck of matter, and the crash of worlds."
Scriptures that tell of the earth passing away and perishing never speak of annihilation, but of transition. (Cf: 2 Pet. 3:10, 12-13).

2. IT IS TO UNDERGO GREAT PHYSICAL CHANGES.
This is anticipated in the Millennial Period., (Ps. 72. Ps. 65:9-13. Isa. 35).

3. IT IS TO BECOME A PERFECT PLACE OF HABITATION.

Cf. its present loveliness; but then, by means of Redemption (Rom: 8:21) it will become *"the Garden of God."*

III. THE MORAL CONDITION OF EARTH'S INHABITANTS WILL BE NEW.

1. THERE WILL BE ONLY REDEEMED PEOPLE ON EARTH.

"Them that are saved" (Rev. 21:2). (Also, 1 Pet. 3:13b).

These will consist of the saved of all nations, who came through the Millennial Age.

The "Kingdom" they will inherit is not the Millennial, but the Eternal.

2. THERE WILL NEVER BE FREEDOM FROM ALL EVIL INFLUENCE.

Satan and all the unsaved have received *"their part"* in the *"lake of fire"* (Rev. 20:10-15. 21:8).

3. THERE WILL BE PERFECT FRATERNITY BETWEEN ALL NATIONS.

Verse 24. National life will be perpetuated but all national rivalries and barriers will be broken down.

IV. THE REGULAR COURSE OF HUMAN EXPERIENCE WILL BE NEW.

1. THERE WILL BE NO MORE SUFFERING (21:4).

Tears and pain are done away. Contrast our present estate. (The word *"wipe away"* occurs only here and in 7:17 and means that the very fountain of men's tears will be stanched).

2. THERE WILL BE NO MORE DEATH (4).

Corpses, coffins, grave stones, and cemeteries will be no more. No more death beds: no more sad farewells.
And all this because,

3. THERE WILL BE NO MORE SIN.

Suffering, sorrow, and death are the effects of Sin; and these effects will be no more, because the Cause will be no more.

SFO Notes

Insert verse verification.

OUTLINE NO. 14
Babylon in History and Prophecy
(Rev. 17 & 18)

I. THE INTERPRETATION OF THE "WOMAN"

IS THE SUBJECT OF BOTH THESE CHAPTERS (17 & 18)
Is the same place or thing meant in each case?
Two answers:--

1. No. Chapter 17—Symbolic
i.e. Papal Rome.
Chapter 18. Actual B i.e. in Chaldea.

2. Yes. Two presentations of one thing, Babylon
a. On several grounds must be rejected.
b. Is correct but is this B symbolic? Or literal?
Answer: Both (cf 17:1-5 and 18, with 17:18).
17:18 pointing back interprets the symbolic account:
pointing on interprets the literal account.

But if the same thing, B is meant in both Chapters one
symbolic, the other literal.
What are we to understand by Babylon?
Two Views:
a. Rome: in chapter 17 Papal, the Church of Rome.
b. Babylon: in chapter 17:18 the City
(ch. 17)–Mystical
(ch 18)–Literal

CHAPTER 17	CHAPTER 18
A WOMAN	A CITY
A PRINCIPAL	A PLACE
A SYSTEM	A CENTER
RELIGIOUS	CIVIL
B: MORALLY	B: MATERIALLY
ECCLESIASTICAL	POLITICAL
BABYLONIANISM	BABYLON

II. THE ORIGIN OF BABYLON.

(Rev. 10: 8-11).

III. THE DESTINY OF BABYLON.

1. The System. (17:15-17).
2. The City. (18).

IV. THE REVIVAL OF BABYLON.

Is the city to be rebuilt?[3]
Yes, because,

1. The predictions of its destruction have not yet been fulfilled.
(Cf: Isa. 13:19,20. Jer. 50:1-3,40,46. Jer. 51:26,29, 43. 61-64.)
Inhabited: Hillah, population: 10,000.

2. The predictions of its revival have not yet been fulfilled.
(Zech. 5). Written after ancient Babylon was destroyed.
(Rev. 18). Gentile World-history will end where it began, in the land of Shinar.

IV. THE FUTURE POWER OF BABYLON. COMMERCIAL. IS THE RE-BUILDING OF BABYLON POSSIBLE AND LIKELY?

(Here Dr. Scroggie quotes a magazine of his day, *"Daily Express"* on this likelihood. Scroggie lived long enough to witness this rebuilding stage of the Middle-East but died before this region became "Oil-Powerful," EAJ).

SFO Notes

Give verse numbers and write out sermon in full to show the flow of truth.

---

3 Author's note. Scroggie wrote this around 1918 at a time when the Middle East was a vast uninfluential desert; long before the re-establishment of the Nation of Israel; far before the dominance of the Oil Cartel and the prominence of the Arab nations. In 1918 the thought of a powerful and world- threatening Iraq was inconceivable. EAJ.

5
Notes on:
The Kingdom, the Lord's Return, Sayings from the Cross.

NOTES NO. 1

Ideas resident in the terms: Kingdom, mixed; Church, select.

I. THE KINGDOM.

The kingdoms of Scripture: God, Messiah, Heavens.

II. THE CHURCH.

The fact of the Kingdom revelation: Suffering, Glory, (Luke 24:26. 1 Pet. 1:11)

The Church comes between these two, and, consequently, is not predicted in the O. T.
For the Church period see Hosea 3:4.
"For the children of Israel shall abide many days without a king, and without a prince, and without a sacrifice, and without an image, and without an ephod, and without teraphim."
For the Kingdom period see Hosea 3:5.
"Afterward shall the children of Israel return, and seek the LORD their God, and David their king; and shall fear the LORD and his goodness in the latter days."

III. THE ADVENTS.

Relation to Kingdom and Church. The latter falls in time between 1st and 2nd Advents.

NOTES NO. 2
THE LORD'S RETURN
As related to life and service.

The great historical facts of the Lord's life are intended to be spiritual factors of the Christian Life.

A. HIS DEATH AND RESURRECTION
B. HIS INTERCESSION MINISTRY IN HEAVEN
C. HIS CERTAIN COMING AGAIN

THIS LAST TRUTH IS INTENDED TO PROMOTE:

1. PURITY OF CHARACTER
   (1 Jn. 3:2-3; 1 Tim. 6:11; Tit. 2:11-13; Col. 3:4-8, 12-14)

2. WORTHINESS OF WALK
   (Rom. 13: 11-14; Phil. 3:16., 4:1; Eph 4:25, 5:4)

3. PATIENCE UNDER TRIAL
   (Heb. 10:35-36; Jas. 5:7-8; 1 Pet. 1:7, 4:13)

4. COMFORT IN SORROW
   (John 14:1-3; 1 Thess. 4:15-18)

5. PERSISTENCE OF ENDEAVOR
   (2 Tim. 4:7-8)

6. DILIGENCE IN SERVICE
   (1 Cor. 15:58; Phil. 2:16; 1 Thess. 2:19; 2 Tim. 4:1-2; 1 Pet. 5:2-4)

7. WATCHFULNESS OF DISPOSITION
   (1 Thess. 1:9-10; 1 Pet. 4:7)

NOTES NO. 3
Sayings from the Cross
"It is Finished" (John 19:30).

SIXTH OF THE SEVEN SAYINGS FROM THE CROSS

I. BEFORE THE DARKNESS

1. *"Father, forgive them, for they know not what they do"* (Luke 23:34).
2. *"To-day shalt thou be with me in Paradise"* (Luke 23:43).
3. *"Woman, behold thy son!..Behold thy mother"* (John 19:26-27).

II. DURING THE DARKNESS

4. *"My God, my God, why hast thou forsaken Me?"* (Matt. 27:46; Mark 15:34).

III. AFTER THE DARKNESS

5. *"I thirst"* (John 19:28).
6. *"It is finished"* (John 19:30).
7. *"Father, into Thy hands I commend my spirit"* (Luke 23:46).

"It is begun"— "It is going on" — "It is finished"—of any task.

1. THAT THE EARTHLY LIFE OF CHRIST HAD COME TO ITS CLOSE
The reason for living was now over, and nothing remained for Him but to die.

2. THAT CHRIST'S OBEDIENCE TO THE FATHER WAS NOW PERFECTED

The Law fulfilled. Humiliation and submission complete. (Phil. 2).

3. THAT THE WORK CHRIST CAME TO DO WAS NOW ACCOMPLISHED

4. THAT THE O.T. PROPHECIES CONCERNING CHRIST WERE NOW FULFILLED

Seed of woman. Passover (Isa. 53). Smite the Shepherd.

5. THAT THE HUMAN SUFFERINGS OF CHRIST WERE NOW AT AN END

6. THAT PERFECT DIVINE ATONEMENT FOR SIN WAS NOW FOREVER MADE

Redemption-Salavtion-Sonship—Fellowship—Holiness-Glory.

7. THAT THE UNIVERSAL SOVEREIGNTY OF CHRIST WAS NOW ESTABLISHED

Over Sin, Death, Devil. As at the end of a book—*Finis.*

LESSONS

A. Within the limits of our short life, there is given to each of us a work to do.

B. No work which is not Divinely given to us can ever be finished.

C. The Sacrifice of Christ makes possible to us all, the joy of accomplishment.

PRAISE BE THINE!
I see the whole design,
I, who saw power, see love now perfect too.
Perfect I call thy Man.
Thanks that I was a man!
Make, remake, complete.
I trust what thou shalt do.

—Rabbi Ben Ezra

NOTES NO. 4
Notes Missionary
The Missionary Venture
(Isa. 55: 12-13)

Introduction: The Primary and Ultimate Application.

I. THE CALL. *"Ye shall go out ... and be led forth."*

   1. IT IS A GOING OUT.
   2. IT IS A BEING LED FORTH.

II. THE EQUIPMENT. *"With joy and with peace."*

   1. WITH THE JOY OF ANTICIPATION.
   2. WITH THE PEACE OF ASSURANCE.

III. THE TASK. *"Mountains, hills, thorns, briars."*

   1. THERE ARE DIFFICULTIES
   2. THERE ARE ENEMIES

IV. THE PROMISE.

   1. OF JUBILATION
   2. OF TRANSFORMATION

SFO Notes

Verse verification!

NOTES NO. 5
Notes Missionary
The Missionary Enterprise
(Mark 16:15; Matt. 28:20)

"Having gone into all the world, proclaiming the Glad Tidings to all the creation."

"And, lo, I am with you alway, even unto the end of the world."

I. THE COMMAND.

    1. THE OUTLOOK—*"All the world."*
    2. THE OBLIGATION— *"Go ye into."*

II. THE TASK.

    1. ITS NATURE— *"Preach the Gospel."*
    2. ITS INCLUSIVENESS—*"to every creature."*

III. THE PROMISE

    1. CHRIST'S PERSONAL PRESENCE—*"Lo, I am with you alway."*
    2. CHRIST'S ABIDING PRESENCE—*"Until the end."*

SFO Notes

Include verse numbers.

NOTES FROM ROMANS

NOTES NO. 6.
The Two Adams
(Rom. 5:12-21)

INTRODUCTION.

I. THEIR DIVINE ORIGIN.

    1. THE FIRST ADAM, (GEN. 2:7).
      A. THE BODY FORMED.
      B. THE SPIRIT INBREATHED.
      C. THE SOUL CONSTITUTED.

    2. THE LAST ADAM.
      A. PREDICTED BY THE PROPHETS.
      B. DECLARED BY THE EVANGELISTS.
      C. ASSUMED BY THE APOSTLES.

II. THEIR UNIQUE POSITION.

    1. THE FIRST ADAM.
      A. THE HEAD OF A NATURAL RACE.
      B. THE TYPICAL MAN OF HIS RACE.
      C. THE FINAL EXPRESSION OF HIS RACE.

    2. THE LAST ADAM.
      A. THE HEAD OF A SPIRITUAL RACE.
      B. THE TYPICAL MAN OF HIS RACE.
      C. THE FINAL EXPRESSION OF HIS RACE.

III. THEIR DETERMINING WORK.

    1. THE FIRST ADAM.
      A. HIS ONE RUINING ACT.
      B. THE PERSONAL AND IMMEDIATE RESULTS.

C. THE RELATIVE AND ULTIMATE CONSEQUENCES.

2. THE LAST ADAM.
    A. HIS ONE SAVING ACT.
    B. THE PERSONAL AND IMMEDIATE RESULTS.
    C. THE RELATIVE AND ULTIMATE CONSEQUENCES.

SFO Notes

Study Romans 5:21 and fill in with, references, the verification for the homiletical structure outlines here.

NOTES NO. 7
The Resurrection in Romans

The importance of anything may be judged by a consideration of what the situation would be if it were disproved and could no longer be regarded as a fact.

Apply this test to the subject of the Resurrection of Jesus Christ, as it is witnessed to in the Letter to Rome.

IF THE RESURRECTION IS NOT A FACT:

1. JESUS WAS NOT DIVINE, (1:4).

2. THERE IS NO JUSTIFICATION FOR MEN, (4:24,25).

3. THERE IS NO ETERNAL LIFE FOR MEN, (5:10).

4. MAN'S DEDICATION UNTO GOD IS IMPOSSIBLE, (6:1-14).

5. THERE IS NO BRIDEGROOM FOR THE SOUL, (7:4).

6. THERE WILL BE NO QUICKENING FOR THE BODY, (8:2).

7. WE HAVE NO HIGH PRIEST IN HEAVEN, (8:34).

8. THERE IS NO WAY OF SALVATION, (10:9).

9. THERE IS NO LORDSHIP OVER THE DEAD AND THE LIVING, (14:9).

NOTES NO. 8
The Wage and the Gift
(Rom. 6:23)

THE PAIRS OF CONTRASTS:
SIN AND GOD, DEATH AND LIFE, WAGES AND GIFT.

I. *"The wages of sin is death."*

A. THE LORDSHIP OF SIN.

1. There are operating in the world but two moral principles: Sin and Righteousness, (18-20).

2. Each of us is in the service of the one or the other, (16b). Means of necessity directed by some principle.

3. The one which we obey is the one of our choice and is our master, (13:16a, 19).
As free moral beings we must and do choose.

B. THE TERRORS OF DEATH.

1. Physical death. The separation of the soul from the body.

2. Spiritual death. The separation of the soul and body forever from God.

3. Eternal death. The separation of the soul and body forever from God.

C. THE PAYMENT OF WAGES.

1. The logical relation between Death and Sin. It is "wages" due and in justice paid.

2. The 'wage' is in part paid as the work is done. 'Death' is a penal evil so that all the consequences of sin here and now belong to death.

3. The full reward of sin is at the end of man's probation here. The sinner will then receive in full the wages due to him from sin.

II. *"The free gift of God is Eternal Life in Christ Jesus our Lord".*

A. THE BLESSINGS OF LIFE.

1. Eternal life is recovery of the life forfeited by sin—physical and spiritual.

2. Eternal life is more than the recovery of what was lost; it is Divine Life.

3. Eternal life is not only a future but a present blessing.
"I give unto my sheep," "this is life eternal."

B. THE GIFT OF GOD.

1. This life cannot be earned. It is not a *'wage.'*

2. This life is offered on the ground of Grace. *"I give."*

3. This life must be appropriated by faith. *"Through faith, and not of yourselves."*

C. THE SPHERE OF ENJOYMENT.

1. It is in Christ—Who was the manifold life of God.

2. It is in Jesus—Who died that we might live.

3. It is in the Lord—Who lives to be our life.

We must, serve either Sin or Righteousness. Either earn a

"wage", or receive a "gift."

Either eternally die, or eternally live. *"Choose ye this day."*

NOTES FROM MATTHEW

NOTES NO. 9
Forgiveness: Divine & Human
(Matt. 18:23-35)

INTRODUCTION (21-22).

I. THE KING'S TREATMENT OF HIS SERVANT, (23-27).

1. The Reckoning, (23).
2. The Debtor, (24,25a).
3. The Punishment, (25b).
4. The Appeal, (26).
5. The Mercy, (27).

II. THE SERVANT'S TREATMENT OF HIS FELLOW., (28-34).

1. The Indebtedness, (28a).
2. The Demand, (28b).
3. The Entreaty, (29).
4. The Refusal, (30).
5. The Consequences, (31-34).

NOTES NO. 10
First Things First in Matthew

1. FIRST INWARD PURITY AND THEN OUTWARD PROPRIETY, (23:26).

> *"Thou blind Pharisee, cleanse first that which is within the cup and platter, that the outside of them may be clean also."*

2. FIRST REFORM OF SELF AND THEN REPROOF OF OTHERS, (7:5).

> *"Thou hypocrite, first cast out the beam out of thine own eye; and then shalt thou see clearly to cast out the mote out of thy brother's eye."*

3. FIRST ADJUSTMENT WITH MEN AND THEN APPROACH TO GOD, (5:24).

> *"Leave there thy gift before the altar, and go thy way: first be reconciled to thy brother, and then come and offer thy gift."*

4. FIRST TRUE (WIDESPREAD) GODLINESS AND THEN TEMPORAL (WORLDLY) GOOD, (6:33).

> *"But seek ye first the kingdom of God, and his righteousness, and all these things shall be added unto you."*

5. FIRST THE SAVIOR'S CALL AND THEN SOCIAL CLAIMS, (8:21).

> *"And another of his disciples said unto him, Lord, suffer me first to go and bury my father."*

NOTES NO. 11
The Two—Category Truth

1. THE TWO FOUNDATIONS, (Matt. 7:24-27).
Rock and Sand.

2. THE TWO WAYS, (Matt. 7:13-14).
Broad and Narrow.

3. THE TWO MASTERS, (Matt. 6:24).
God and the World.

4. THE TWO DESCRIPTIONS, (Mark)
Whole and Sick. Righteous and Sinners.

5. THE TWO RELATIONS.
Children of God; and of the Devil.
(John 1:12, 11:52; Gal. 3:26; Rom. 8:14,16; 1 Jn. 3:1-2, 3:10; Matt. 13:38; John 8:44; Acts 13:10; 1 Jn. 3:8).

6. THE TWO STATES, (Luke 19:10).
Lost and Saved.

7. THE TWO DESTINIES, (Matt. 7:13,14. 13:47-50. 25:46).
Destruction and Life.

NOTES NO. 12
The Virgins & The Servants
(Matt. 25:1-13, 14-30)

TWO ASPECTS OF THE CHRISTIAN LIFE.

VIRGINS.	**SERVANTS.**
1. Women. Ten.	Men. Three.
2. 5 and 5.	2 and 1.
3. All who profess Christ: Real, 5: false, 5.	All who profess Christ: Real, 2: false, 1.
4. Waiting for Christ to come.	Working till Christ does come.
5. Inward life; the Contemplative	Outward activity; the Energetic.
6. Warning against Indifference.	Warning against Indolence.
7. Too easy-to serve the Lord	The melancholy Christian.
8. The sanguine Christian.	One erred through under-confidence.
9. Five erred through overconfidence.	Not risking enough.

FIRST CHARACTER　　　　**THEN SERVICE**

SFO Notes

Excellent comparative study. Find and add verification verses and write out in full sermon form.

NOTES NO. 13
The Pearl
(Matt. 13:45-46)

"Again, the kingdom of heaven is like unto a merchant man, seeking goodly pearls: who, when he had found one pearl of great price, went and sold all that he had, and bought it."

1. SEEKING.
>The Eternal Desire: REVELATION.

2. FINDING.
>The Mystical Discovery: ANTICIPATION.

3. SELLING.
>The Historical Descent: INCARNATION.

4. BUYING.
>The Sacrificial Death: CRUCIFIXION.

SFO Notes

Read and reread the parable and add verification verses and application.

NOTES FROM MARK

NOTES NO. 14
Till He Come
(Mark 13:33-37)

INTRODUCTION—OCCASION

I. A DESIGN IS REVEALED, (34).

1. A purpose to depart.
2. A purpose to tarry.
3. A purpose to return.

II. A DUTY IS ENJOINED, (33,35,37).

1. To work.
2. To watch.
3. To pray.

III. A DANGER IS DISCLOSED, (36).

1. Sinful indolence.
2. Dreamy unconcern.
3. Shameful insensibility.

SFO Notes

Study the passage and add verification and applications.

NOTES NO. 15
What?
(Mark 10:51)

"What wilt thou that I should do unto thee?"
"What do you want me to do for you?" (RSV).

I. JESUS IMPLIES.

1. That we stand in NEED of something.
2. That we are CONSCIOUS of our need.
3. That we are HELPLESS to meet our need.
4. That we WANT our need to be met.
5. That He ALONE can meet our need.

II. JESUS APPEALS.

1. To our spiritual UNDERSTANDING.
2. To our SINCERITY of heart.
3. To our sense of URGENCY.
4. To our faculty of FAITH.
5. To our WILL to be blessed.

SFO Notes

Good gospel story; read it carefully and add verification references and their evangelistic application.

NOTES NO. 16
The Power of Passionate Prayer
(Mark 1:40)

"And there came a leper to him, beseeching him, and kneeling down to him, and saying unto him, If thou wilt, thou canst make me clean."

1. EXPECTANT
   "He came."

2. REVERENT
   "He knelt."

3. EARNEST
   "He besought."

4. IMMEDIATE
   "To Jesus."

5. DEFINITE
   "Make clean."

6. PERSONAL
   "Me."

7. SUBMISSIVE
   "If Thou wilt."

8. CONFIDENT
   "Thou canst."

9. BRIEF
   Five words.

10. EFFECTUAL
   He was cleansed.

SFO Notes

Mark 1:40 and context and fill in reference numbers.

NOTES NO. 17
(Mark 4:26-29)

INTRODUCTION:
  A. THE THREE HUSBANDRY PARABLES
   1. Soils. 2. Tares. 3. Seed.

  B. THE SEED AND TARES PARABLES
   Tares—emphasizing beginning and end.
   Seed—emphasizing the process between.

  C. THE SEED AND SOILS PARABLES
   Soils—large responsibility of those who hear.
   Seed—limited responsibility of those who proclaim.

I. THE SIMPLE BEGINNINGS OF SPIRITUAL LIFE IN THE SOUL, (26).
   A. THE LIVING SEED. "seed"
   B. THE FAITHFUL SOWING. "a man should cast"
   C. THE RECEPTIVE SOIL. "unto the ground"

II. THE MYSTERIOUS PROCESSES OF SPIRITUAL LIFE IN THE SOUL, (27-28).
   A. THE SPONTANEOUS GROWTH OF THE SEED.
   B. THE GRADUAL PERFECTING OF THE SEED.
   C. THE ORDERLY DEVELOPMENT OF THE SEED.

III. THE WONDERFUL ISSUES OF SPIRITUAL LIFE IN THE SOUL, (29).
   A. THE RIPENED FRUIT—*"the fruit is brought forth."*
   B. THE REAPING SICKLE—*"he putteth in the sickle."*
   C. THE HARVEST NOW—*"the harvest is come."*

Conclusion:
   1. FAITHFUL SOWING
   2. PATIENT WAITING
   3. JOYFUL REWARD

NOTES FROM LUKE

NOTES NO. 18
The Ten Lepers
(Luke 17:11-19)

INTRODUCTION:

1. A FRATERNITY OF WOE, (12).
2. A DARING VENTURE, (12-13).
3. AN EXACTING TEST, (14a).
4. AN INESTIMABLE BLESSING, (14b).
5. AN APPALLING NEGLECT, (17-18).
6. A GRIEVOUS DISAPPOINTMENT, (17).
7. A FITTING ACKNOWLEDGMENT, (15-16).
8. AN ENRICHING FAITH, (19).

SFO Notes

Good gospel message for an evangelistic meeting. Study the passage and fill in actual words for each reference, and the necessary application.

NOTES NO. 19
At Jesus' Feet in Luke

The place for all:

1. WHO ARE SICK OF SIN, (7:38).
(The woman who was a sinner)
There the penitent receive pardon.

2. WHO ARE YOUNG IN THE FAITH, (8:35).
(The Gadarene demonic)
There the weak are safe-guarded.

3. WHO HAVE A BURDEN OF GRIEF, (8:41).
(Jairus, the ruler, about his "one only daughter")
There the stricken are comforted.

4. WHO WOULD KNOW GOD, (10:39).
(Mary of Bethany)
There the eager are taught.

5. WHO ARE THANKFUL OF HEART, (17:16)
(The Samaritan leper)
There the grateful are further blessed.

NOTES NO. 20
Luke 7:37-38

The pathway of this woman into fullness of blessing.

1. CONSCIOUSNESS OF GUILT.

2. EXERCISE OF FAITH.

3. ASSURANCE OF PARDON.

4. SENSE OF PURITY.

5. UPWELLING OF LOVE.

6. EXPRESSION OF GRATITUDE.

7. INHERITANCE OF PEACE.

8. NECESSITY OF SERVICE
   (MINISTRY OF WITNESS)

SFO Notes

To ensure that your listeners follow the "pathway to fulness of blessing" you need to fill in the relevant verses and sequence for flow of the story. Be sure to write the sermon in full for your own mastery of the eight points.

NOTES NO. 21
The Nature of the Gospel
(Luke 2:8-14)

I. THE NATURE OF THE GOSPEL.

    A. ITS GENESIS IS HISTORIC
    Time
    Place
    Circumstance

    B. ITS MESSAGE IS REDEMPTIVE.
    A Savior
    Christ the Lord

II. THE UNIVERSALITY OF THE GOSPEL.

    A. IT IS INDISCRIMINATE IN ITS APPEAL.
    Shepherds
    Simple
    Poor

    B. IT IS COMPREHENSIVE IN ITS SCOPE.
    All people

III. THE EFFECT OF THE GOSPEL.
    A. IT BANISHES FEAR
    "Fear not."

    B. IT GENERATES JOY
    "Great joy."

SFO Notes

This is an excellent outline for a Christmas message. So use it with all the points covered by verifying verses and necessary transitions. Plus applications. Write out the sermon in full and preach it often at the appropriate time of the year!

NOTES NO. 22
The Redeeming Mission
Luke 19:10

"For the Son of man is come to seek and to save that which is lost."

I. THE BRINGER OF SALVATION, "Son of man"

   1. AS TO NATURE.
     A. GOD—REQUIRING SATISFACTION.
     B. MAN—SECURING SATISFACTION.

   2. AS TO OFFICE.
     A. PROPHET—BRINGING THE DIVINE MESSAGE TO US.
     B. PRIEST—REPRESENTING HUMAN NEED OF GOD.
     C. KING—POSSESSING UNIVERSAL, SOVEREIGN POWER.

II. THE OBJECTS OF SALVATION, The *"lost."*

   1. WHAT IS MEANT BY BEING *"LOST."*
     A. MONEY STOLEN OR MISLAID.
     B. BUILDING RUINED.
     C. SHIP WRECKED.
     D. TRAVELERS OUT OF THE WAY.
     E. PERSON DEAD.

   2. IN WHAT SENSE CAN MEN BE *"LOST."*
     A. SOCIALLY.
     B. WILLFULLY.
     C. UNCONSCIOUSLY.
     D. HEREDITARILY.
     E. ETERNALLY.

III. THE NATURE OF SALVATION, "Save."
   1. CLEANING FROM THE GUILT OF SIN.
   2. CLEANSING FROM DEFILEMENT OF SIN.
   3. FORGIVENESS FOR THE CRIME OF SIN.

4. DELIVERANCE FROM THE POWER OF SIN.
5. REMOVAL OF THE LOVE OF SIN.

IV. THE METHOD OF SALVATION, *"to seek."*
  1. BY LOSSES.
  2. BY SUFFERINGS.
  3. BY MERCIES.
  4. BY THE GOSPEL.
  5. BY THE SPIRIT.

V. THE SUCCESS (FRUITS) OF SALVATION. Types reached.
  1. SAUL THE SCHOLAR, (Acts 9).
  2. JOSEPH THE WEALTHY, (John 19).
  3. CORNELIUS THE SOLDIER, (Acts 10).
  4. THE UNNAMED THIEF, (Luke 23).
  5. THE PROFLIGATE WOMAN, (Luke 7).
  6. NICODEMUS THE THINKER, (John 3).
  7. ZACCHAEUS THE TAX COLLECTOR, (Luke 19).

People 'down and out' to 'up and out'.

SFO Notes

This outline is so full that it might be best to preach it in five sequential occasions (or weeks). It will need a lot of work to support the many points under the respective headings of "Son of Man"; the "lost"; "save"; and types reached. But there are Scriptural passages or verses to verify and substantiate each of the sub-headings.

NOTES NO. 23
Aspects of Salvation
Luke 15:20-24

1. THE KISS—FORGIVENESS, RECEPTION (REUNION)
2. THE ROBE—RIGHTEOUSNESS, ROBE
3. THE RING—ASSURANCE, HOLY SPIRIT, RING
4. THE SHOES—SERVICE, RESPONSIBILITY
5. THE FESTIVAL—REJOICING

SUSTENANCE.

FELLOWSHIP.

JOY.

SFO Notes

This is the beloved parable of the lost son. To preach it in context will require an introductory "lead in" of verses 14-19. The aspect of salvation dealt with in this outline is "The Welcome Home"!

Make use of each aspect of the welcome with verse verification–maintaining, at the same time, flow of the story and it's powerful application.

NOTES FROM JOHN

NOTES NO. 24
When He is Come
(John 16:8)

"And when he is come, he will reprove the world of sin, and of righteousness, and of judgment."

1. THE PERSONALITY OF THE SPIRIT.
   A. TERMS.
   B. QUALITIES.
   C. OPERATIONS.
   D. SENSIBILITIES.

2. THE DEITY OF THE SPIRIT.
   A. ASSOCIATIONS.
   B. ATTRIBUTES.
   C. ACTIONS.

3. THE FUNCTION OF THE SPIRIT.
   A. REVEAL.
   B. INTERPRET.
   C. GLORIFY.

4. THE IMPARTMENT OF THE SPIRIT.
   AS: Gift, Sealing, Indwelling, Earnest, Baptism, Filling, Anointing.

5. THE RECEPTION OF THE SPIRIT.
   A. MEANING.
   B. EXPERIENCE.
   C. CONDITIONS.

6. THE EVIDENCES OF THE SPIRIT.
   A. INWARD.
   B. OUTWARD

7. THE CLAIM OF THE SPIRIT

SFO Notes

Here is a basic outline on the Person and Work of the Holy Spirit. It is best treated as a series of studies over seven weeks–at least–after reading carefully John, chapters 14-16; relevant verses in Romans 8, Galatians, and Ephesians.

Verification of Scripture for every point is absolutely vital. Clarity and simplicity with a subject like this must be a priority!

NOTES NO. 25
Jesus is the Answer
(John 3-4)

1. THE SPHERE OF HIS ACTIVITY IS INCLUSIVE.

JUDEA: (3).
SAMARIA: (4:1-42).
GALILEE: (4:43-54).

Regarding the land as a miniature of the world, He takes the whole of it to His heart.

2. THE PEOPLE HE HELPS ARE REPRESENTATIVE.

A man. Jews. Pharisee. Temple.
A woman. Samaritan. Adulterer. Street
A child. Roman. Nobleman. Court.

3. THE DIFFICULTIES HE DEALS WITH ARE COMPREHENSIVE.

Intellectual Perplexity—MIND
Moral Insensibility—CONSCIENCE
Emotional Anxiety—HEART

4. THE MANNER OF HIS TREATMENT IS DISCRIMINATING.

Nicodemus–appeal to Scripture. (Ezek. 36:25-27; 37:9).
Woman–appeal to Conscience. (John 4:16).
Nobleman–appeal to Faith. (John 4:50).

5. THE REVELATION HE VOUCHSAFES IS SATISFYING.
To each of these He reveals Himself; as

LIFE To NICODEMUS.
LIGHT To THE WOMAN
LOVE To THE NOBLEMAN

NOTES NO. 26
True Worship
(John 4:21-24)

THE CONTEXT.

I. THE OBJECT OF TRUE WORSHIP—GOD

  A. WHO IS SPIRIT.
  B. WHO IS FATHER.

    cf: Idolatry–false and transient.
    Judaism–true and temporary.
    Christianity–full and final.

II. THE NATURE OF TRUE WORSHIP—Spiritual

  A. IN SPIRIT: ESSENCE OF PERSONALITY. cf: sensuous.
  B. IN TRUTH: ESSENCE OF REALITY. cf: partial and false.
    Jew, Samaritan.

III. THE UNIVERSALITY OF TRUE WORSHIP.

  A. IN ALL RACES.
  B. AT ALL TIMES.

IV. THE MEANS OF TRUE WORSHIP.

  A. PRIVATE DEVOTIONS.
    1. Scriptures
    2. Prayer

  B. PUBLIC FELLOWSHIP
    1. Song.

2. Preaching.
3. Lord's table.

V. THE REASONS OF TRUE WORSHIP
A. THE NATURE OF THE MAN.
Our capacity for God.

B. THE SEARCH OF GOD.
Why and how He seeks.

WHOM: GOD, FATHER, SPIRIT
HOW: SPIRIT
WHEN: ALL TIMES
WHERE: EVERYWHERE

SFO Notes

People in our churches, today, are hopelessly confused as to the nature of TRUE WORSHIP. With confirming Scripture for each point and attention to the "flow" of truth, with appropriate transitions, this can be delivered as ONE expository sermon.

PART TWO
Sermons of W. Graham Scroggie

6

His Sermon Preparation
(Comments by E. A. Johnston)

The preparation of a sermon outline for Graham Scroggie was akin to crafting a masterpiece! His approach to sermon preparation was as thorough and erudite as if it were his last sermon on this earth. Moreover, his attention to detail is evident in his careful homiletical style, which he laid out with different colored inks to emphasize his expository outlines. A typical Scroggie sermon outline has the look of an artist's canvas with its varying colors and bold strokes. One can picture him at his desk with open Bible and commentary, and within reach are his different colored pens and pencils ready for employment. When one goes through his hand-written papers there is a noticeable precision to Dr. Scroggie! With Edinburgh often referred to as the "Athens of Scotland", it is apparent that Graham Scroggie did not "dumb down" the academic climate of his sermons for his hearers (as we sometimes do today). Quite the contrary He often gave his audience a Greek lesson while bringing forth his centralizing theme wrapped up in its unifying thoughts and the motivational thrust of his dynamic message. From a sample sermon outline in his hand entitled, "The Christian and Evil" from the text of 1 Corinthians 5:6 and 2 Corinthians 5:7, he comments atop the page,

"There is doctrine in the N. T. grammar–the phrase

is in the Aorist tense, the Imperative Mood, the Active Voice.

A) Mood = Imperative = the need is urgent.

B) Tense = Aorist = the action must be instantaneous and complete

C) Voice = Active = the operation must be our own and not another's."

Graham Scroggie had a remarkable career as pastor, author, Bible teacher, and preacher. He was a meticulous individual who kept precise files for his notes, outlines, and sermons. In the "Scroggie Collection," maintained by Olford Ministries, is a history of the times, as well as studies in homiletics. There are stacks and stacks of large envelopes filled with not only Dr. Scroggie's hand written work, but also with historic church bulletins and newspapers from both the First and Second World Wars. The library of sermonic material is vast. Hence we have tried to give the reader a "taste" of his genius as a preacher and homiletician, choosing sermons which we felt were fair representations of the man. Although there remains a large amount of unpublished work by Scroggie, we hope the following sermons by him are helpful to preachers and teachers today.

Many of these selected sermons were preached while Dr. Scroggie was the pastor of the Metropolitan Tabernacle in London, England. Therefore it is fitting to take some time to elaborate on the Metropolitan Tabernacle and Dr. Scroggie's influence while pastor there during the years of World War Two. Built by C. H. Spurgeon to accommodate his growing congregation, the original building was completed before the spring of 1861 and held its opening service on March 18, 1861. During this same year the war between the Union and the Confederacy broke out in America. But in London, on that particular Sunday in March the "Gov'nor" took the pulpit and dedicated the church building to God. The massive structure could easily seat between 5,000 to 6,000 people. In 1898 (six years after Spurgeon's death) the original structure burned to the ground. When the church was rebuilt under the direction of Spurgeon's son, Tom, the seating capacity was reduced to around 4,000. By the time W. Graham Scroggie became the Pastor of the Metropolitan Tabernacle it had seen its once overflowing congregation diminish with the downgrade of church attendance by the end of World War Two. Today, the church accommodates around 800 to 900 people. Graham Scroggie had heard Spurgeon preach on many occasions. In fact, Scroggie was a lad of fifteen when the "Prince of Preachers" died. Dr. W. Graham Scroggie preached his first sermon at the Metropolitan in March of 1918. Spurgeon's influence on Scroggie is seen in the fact that four years after Spurgeon's death, Graham Scroggie enrolled at Spurgeon's College at the age of 19 to begin training for the ministry, graduating a few years later. It was only fitting that the pulpit of the great Metropolitan Tabernacle was filled by W. Graham Scroggie between the years 1938 to 1944. Scroggie commanded respect in the pulpit, and as a Bible teacher and homiletician he had few equals.

As Pastor of the Metropolitan Tabernacle, Graham Scroggie maintained a pulpit that brought honor both to the church and to the memory of its founder, C. H. Spurgeon. The messages he preached there have been lost to history until now. Olford Ministries now reintroduces these sermonic "jewels" for today's ministers around the world. We will begin the second part of this volume of OLFORD ON SCROGGIE with three outstanding sermons which Graham Scroggie preached at the Metropolitan. The first sermon is entitled, "THE MANIFESTO OF SPIRITUAL WORSHIP." It was the first sermon Dr. Scroggie preached after he had become the Pastor of the Metropolitan Tabernacle. The text is John 4:21-24 concerning the woman at the well in Samaria. It was preached on February 6th, 1938. The second sermon is entitled, "HISTORY AND PROPHECY MEET" and the text for it is Matthew 11:23-34 regarding Jesus' prediction of coming judgment on Capernaum. This message was preached in March of 1918! The third message is historical and was deeply moving for the congregation at the time; it was preached amid the ruins of the Metropolitan which had been destroyed by German bombers on May 11, 1941. Scroggie's message is tenderly entitled, "SPURGEON, 1834-1892," and he preached it on June 6th, 1941, literally in the rubble as he and the grieving congregation stood knee deep in the ruins of their beloved church!

These messages are historic, profound, and fitted for the occasions like shining jewels in a ring of gold. We hope that you are blessed by them and that you can make use of them for the glory of God and for the good of His people.

7

The Manifesto
of Spiritual Worship

"Jesus saith unto her, Woman, believe me, the hour cometh, when ye shall neither in this mountain, nor yet at Jerusalem, worship the Father. Ye worship ye know not what: we know what we worship: for salvation is of the Jews. But the hour cometh, and now is, when the true worshippers shall worship the Father in spirit and in truth: for the Father seeketh such to worship him. God is a spirit: and they that worship him must worship him in spirit and in truth" (John 4:21-24).

The passage which we have read is one of the profoundest in the teaching of our Lord, and the circumstances of its utterance are scarcely less wonderful. Not to a company of intellectuals, philosophical, or religious, did Christ communicate this profoundest truth of ethic and religion—"a truth which no sage in the East or West had ever surpassed, and towards which the highest minds in all the ages of Christendom have been slowly making approach"—but to a woman, a Samaritan woman, a woman who was living an immoral life. It is to such an one that He said, *"God is Spirit, and they that worship Him must worship Him in spirit and truth."* In this utterance we have what has been called "The Manifesto of Spiritual Worship," and we cannot do better than to closely contemplate it for a while. And to begin with, let us consider:

I. THE IDEA OF TRUE WORSHIP

We are told that–

"The word first appears among the Greeks after their contact with the Persians, and is employed by the poets for profoundly reverential worship of the gods, and supplication of them." Its meaning in the Old Testament may be gathered from the various translations of it in our versions.

In 2 Kings 17:36 we read, *"Him shall ye worship"*;

In 2 Samuel 9:6, *"Mephibosheth fell on his face and did reverence."*

In Exodus 11:8, *"All these thy* (Pharaoh's) *servants shall bow down themselves unto me* (Moses)*"*;

In Genesis 37:7, *"Your sheaves made obeisance to my sheaf."* In Numbers 22:31, *"Balaam fell flat on his face before the Angel"*, and in Proverbs 12:25, *"Heaviness in the heart of man maketh it stoop."*

All these words have one root idea, that of prostration of oneself before another, or others. In the New Testament, a word is employed which is traceable to the oriental custom of throwing a kiss with the hand in token of submission or reverence, and so it comes to mean the devout prostration of the soul before God in humble homage and entire submission. Worship so conceived of, begins, perhaps, in wonder, which deepens into reverence, and is perfected in love. And so the worshipful soul can sing,

"When all Thy mercies, O my God,
My rising soul surveys,
Transported with the view, I'm lost
In wonder, love and praise."

This, then is The Idea of Worship, implicit in the passage before us, and in all others which refer to divine worship. This naturally leads us to consider

II. THE OBJECT OF TRUE WORSHIP

The Bible everywhere declares that the one and only object of worship is the God therein revealed, and nowhere are the Object and obligation revealed more profoundly than in the words of our text, *"God is Spirit, and they that worship Him must worship Him in spirit and in truth–for of a truth the Father seeketh such to worship Him"* (23-24).

"God is Spirit"

Not "a spirit," one of many, but "Spirit", absolutely uncreated, everlasting; the Spirit of all spirits. By this word is revealed the fundamental essence of the Divine Being. The three utterances– "God is Light," "God is Love," and "God is Spirit," are the sublimest ever formed to express the meta-physical, intellectual, and moral essence of the Deity. They are unfathomably deep, and quite inexhaustible in their suggestions. And yet they are not too profound for even a little child or a poor Samaritaness to grasp for practical purposes.

"God is Spirit." The significance of that declaration can never be exhausted. It implies His personality, His non-corporeality, His self-consciousness, His intelligence, His will, and much besides; and as Spirit He is everywhere present, and everywhere active. In the context an inference is drawn from this truth, but, at the moment, it is the truth itself which we should try to grasp. This revelation was not unknown in Israel of old. Solomon in his prayer at the dedication of the temple said:

"Will God indeed dwell on the earth? Behold, the heaven, and heaven of heavens cannot contain Thee, how much less this house that I have builded?" (1 Kgs. 8:27). But, here, Christ presents the truth in a new light, and makes of it a new application. He does this by associating with it what is a distinctive doctrine of the New Covenant, namely, that God is Father.

The thought of the eternal and infinite God, all-holy, all-righteous, all-powerful, in all His greatness and glory, might well overwhelm us and fill us with fear. But when we learn that this Divine Spirit is our Father, our awe is touched with love, and distance melts away. This truth was not unknown in Israel before the Christian era, for Malachi had asked,

"Have we not all one Father?
Hath not one God created us?"

Even a heathen poet had said that men were God's "offspring" (Acts 17:28), but there is a great development of this revelation in the teaching of the New Testament, and especially in the Fourth Gospel. Three times in our text is He spoken of as *"the Father."* The Samaritan woman had said, *"our father Jacob,"* (v. 12), and, *"our fathers worshipped in this mountain"* (v. 20), and Jesus answers her by confronting her with, *"The Father,"* generally by creation, and uniquely by redemption, (vv. 21, 23). He, then, and He alone, the infinite Spirit and the loving Father, is the Object of Worship.

III. THE MANNER OF TRUE WORSHIP

It is this aspect of the subject which gives our text its outstanding significance. The Idea of Worship was not new, and the Object of it was not new, but Christ's word on the Manner of it was startling new. To understand the force of His utterance we must remember that He was talking about two peoples, the Samaritans, and the Jews. Both had knowledge of God, and in both cases that knowledge was partial. Both also had their center and manner of worship. She was a Samaritan, and He was a Jew. The Samaritan center of worship was Mount Gerizim, and the Jewish center was Jerusalem. The religion of the Samaritans was limited and mutilated. They recognized the Pentateuch only, and so cut themselves off from the fuller revelation which came through priests and prophets and psalmists; but *"salvation proceeded from the Jews"* (v. 22). As to their worship, that of the Jews was symbolical and that of the Samaritans was spurious.

All of this is stated or implied in the conversation beside the well, and it occasioned the great revelation of our text. Christ says in effect, "The hour has arrived when worship must be liberated from all limitations of times and places. Henceforth it must be spiritual and not sensuous; universal and not local; enlightened and not ignorant; full and not partial; true and not false." Christ does not say that the Jews' manner of worship was wrong; it was not, for it was divinely appointed, but it was preparatory and disciplinary. The types must now give place to the anti-type; the shadows to the substance; the temporary to the abiding; the symbolic to the spiritual. This does not mean that all times, and places, and forms of worship, are now to be abandoned, but it does mean that unless worship is *"in spirit and in truth"* such times, and places, and forms, are of no use. No matter how sublime the architecture, how elaborate the ritual, how rich the music, how eloquent the preaching, how classic the prayers, if the true spirit of worship be wanting, all else is of no avail.

That is one aspect of the truth, and another is, that in the absence of all these concomitants one can worship God; without Church, or music, or preaching. If this were not true it would be a sad look-out for us, seeing that six-sevenths of our days are spent necessarily in domestic and business pursuits. Does God not require of us worship in the home, and office, and shop; or does He expect it of us on one day a week only, and in a church? Christ answers that inquiry when He says, *"The hour cometh, when neither in Mount Gerizim, nor in Jerusalem, shall ye worship the Father. But the hour cometh and now is, when the true worshippers shall worship the Father in spirit and truth"* (21:23).

> "Spiritual worship is an attitude rather than an act; it is related rather to temper than to time, and to principle than to place. It is not something into which we can project ourselves for occasions, but it is a state of soul, whole-hearted submission to the sovereign, holy, loving will of God; and he who has that spirit must carry it with him into all hours, and places, and occasions; but he who has it not, does not worship at any time or anywhere."

With the coming of Christ, spirituality and reality took the place of symbolism and ignorance; the Jew and the Samaritan gave way to the Christian. Worship, almost necessarily, will express itself in words and forms, but all such derive their value and their power from being the manifestation of spiritual life and spiritual aspiration. The call of God is not for the de-consecration of any place, but for the consecration of every place. What is required of us is not the abandonment of ritual and ceremony, but the spiritualizing of these by making them the expression of a life wholly yielded to God.

"Jesus, where'er Thy people meet,
There they behold Thy mercy seat;
Where'er they seek Thee, Thou art found,
And every spot is hallowed ground!"

Here then, we have plainly indicated what are the Idea, the Object, and the Manner of devotion. But we must get behind these, and ask what is,

IV. THE REASON OF TRUE WORSHIP
That inquiry also is answered in the text:

> *"The true worshippers shall worship the Father in spirit and truth, for the Father also, on His part, or for a truth, the Father seeketh such for His worshippers. God is Spirit, and they that worship Him must worship Him in spirit and truth"* (vv. 23-24).

The reason therefore of true worship is twofold. It is found in what God is, and in what we are. We have already considered the Nature of God. He is Spirit, without bodily parts or passions. That is His eternal Essence, and so He cannot be confined within the limits of time and place. Were He a local deity, the worship of Him would have to be localized; but Infinite Spirit transcends space and time, and calls for a worship which is in keeping with His being. On the other hand, the reason for spiritual worship is to be found in the Nature of Man. We were made "in God's image," with a capacity for Him which inferior creatures do not share. No mere external act of worship can satisfy the human heart. True worship must be personal, and not vicarious; it must be spiritual and not artificial. Just because God is what He is, and because we are what we are, worship must transcend all its possible forms, must overflow all prescribed times, and must be unfettered by all appointed places. To this wonderful revelation Christ adds the further wonder, that, *"The Father seeketh as worshippers those will worship Him in spirit and truth."* There is one other consideration which we must not overlook, though it takes us beyond the scope of the text, namely, the means to true worship.

V. THE MEANS OF TRUE WORSHIP

Let us briefly think of this privilege as exercised in private and public. In Private: our public worship, as to its spirit and manner, will largely reflect our private habit. No one can become spiritual for an occasion. If worship is an attitude, that attitude will be in evidence at all times and everywhere. Now, the spiritual life, like the physical and intellectual, must be cultivated; and the means of its cultivation in private are the Scriptures and prayer. The Word of God must ever be the source of our instruction and inspiration in spiritual things, and only by the constant and careful and responsive reading and study of it can we know the God whom we should worship. And this contact with the Word will inevitably lead to prayer, and the highest form of prayer is worship. The idea that the chief exercise of prayer is petition is a mistake. The chief exercise is the contemplation and adoration of Almighty God. The study of the Scriptures promotes this, and the practice of this promotes the study of the Scriptures. Each reacts upon the other, and out of these proceed all other religious exercises. God cannot be truly worshipped unless and until He is truly known, and He may be known, for He has revealed Himself, but this knowledge can never come except by love and loyalty. As to Worship in Public: While humanly appointed times and places are not essential to worship, they are useful, and necessary if worship is to be social. And here the promoting means are praise and preaching. There is something most uplifting in the singing of a great congregation, in that act of devotion wherein many voices unite to adore the Eternal Spirit. Such an act, if the heart be but right, and the hymn but true, will transport us to the very gates of Heaven. In holy song we spread our wings, and with

> "The whole creation join in one,
> To bless the sacred name,
> Of Him who sits upon the throne,
> And to adore the Lamb."

Then, there is Preaching. If in Praise we speak to God, in

Preaching He speaks to us. If the preacher is really a prophet, then, the people should listen to what is a Divine message, should listen as though Christ Himself were speaking. Prophetic preaching cannot but promote the Spirit of worship, and lead the soul into "wonder, love, and praise." If this, then, be the true character and purpose of public worship, how unseemly a thing it is to disregard the hour of gathering and to saunter in at any time, regardless of the worship of others, and negligent of one's own obligation. If a king summoned us to his court we would not arrive late. For six days a week we take care not to be late at office and shop, but on Sunday, it is only God we are going to meet, so any time will do! But worse still, there are those who, on arrival, do not even strive after the fit and decorous form, who do not bow their heads in prayer, who are not ashamed to be seen looking about them during the most solemn acts of worship, who show that they are indevout, thoughtless, and profane. I trust that this will not be true of any of us, but we shall ever bear in mind that, *"God is Spirit, and they who worship Him must worship Him in spirit and truth."*

8

History and Prophecy Meet

"Thou, Capernaum, which art exalted unto Heaven, shalt be brought down to hell; for if the mighty works which have been done in thee, had been done in Sodom, it would have remained unto this day. But I say unto you that it shall be more tolerable for the land of Sodom in the day of judgment, than for thee." (Matt. 11:23-24)[4]

Our Lord looked back 2,000 years to Sodom and the cities of the Plain, and then He looked out upon His own day and the cities of His time. Then He looked forward prophetically to the cities that would be in the course of history, especially in enlightened places, and He uttered these words with conscious authority. There are two great truths which stand out from all others in these verses.

1. Responsibility is in the Measure of Privilege.

2. Retribution is in the Measure of Responsibility.

Privilege–Responsibility–Retribution. Three great thoughts circle around these three words. Every thoughtful person is looking forward to the future, and trying to read what the future holds for him and for mankind, but the thing that is not

---

4 Author's note (EAJ): the force of this message, preached in 1918, carries with it more meaning with the knowledge that Graham Scroggie's first two churches fired him for the very stance he takes in this powerful message. His first church at Leytonstone, E. London, kicked him out for his opposition to Modernism. The other at Halifax, Yorkshire, fired him for his opposition to worldliness in the church members. Any preacher will face opposition even today for the same stand.

so commonly done is to associate the present with the future, and to realize that what the future holds for you and for me must depend to a large extent on the present. Privilege brings responsibility, and responsibility determines destiny– according to the way it is used. The word responsibility means "ability to respond." What sort of response do we yield?

In Sodom we have the far distant example. Capernaum, a city of our Lord's day, was 2,000 years later. Our own City of London, is representative of other cities of modern times, who have had the same light and the same opportunities. These cities: Sodom–Capernaum–London are separated from one another by about 2,000 years.

I. Responsibility is in the Measure of Privilege.
 A. Notice the different opportunities of these cities.

SODOM did not know very much. Its opportunity was strictly limited to the presence of Lot in the city. He was a converted man, but a backslider. He did not count for much. His chief aim was, not to glorify God, but to make a place for himself, and he succeeded. He sat in the gate–but at the expense of his soul. His witness therefore counted for next to nothing.

CAPERNAUM was exactly the opposite of Sodom for it was in the blaze of light. It had opportunities such as were given to few cities, even in Palestine. It was where our Lord lived. He healed the centurion's servant there, Matthew 8:5. The nobleman's son was cured, John 4:46. Peter's mother-in-law was restored, Mark 1:31. The paralytic was healed, Luke 5:18. The unclean spirit was exorcised there, Mark 1:23. He did mighty things in that place. He spoke mighty words there. He took a child and set him in the midst–a lesson of humility, Matthew 18:2. In the Synagogue at Capernaum He delivered His famous discourse, John 6. In words and works Capernaum was given a supreme opportunity. It was standing in broad daylight compared to Sodom, which was in the dim twilight.

LONDON. Another 2,000 years and we come to our own city. What do we find? If they had a measure of privilege at Sodom, and of great privilege and responsibility at Capernaum, we have supremest opportunity, and greatest and grandest of all privileges in this Christian land, at this late hour in the Christian dispensation, with all the accumulated blessings of the past. Capernaum knew Christ only as the Messiah and miracle worker and teacher. We know Christ as the One who died and rose again and ascended into glory, who has sent His Spirit and has given us His Word–and has built His Church. He has been building it during 1,900 years by mighty operations amongst people in a series of revivals and outpourings of grace and of the accumulated riches of all the years that have gone. We have come into a vast spiritual heritage; our opportunity is a much greater than Capernaum's, as Capernaum's was than Sodom's.

B. Then note the corresponding attitudes which these cities assume to their opportunities.

They have light in different degrees, truth in different measure–but they all assume the same attitude towards light and towards truth. Sodom's opportunity was small but neglected. Capernaum's opportunity was great but it remained obstinate to the last in neglecting Christ. Most of His mighty works were performed there, but they refused Him. London and the cities of today are treating Christ very much worse. The cities of modern Christendom are crucifying Christ afresh, and are putting Him to open shame. We not only neglect His message; we not only pass Him by; we not only remain in unbelief; we are doing worse because theirs was an uncrucified Christ. They did not know what we know; they had not the Bible as we have now; was not in their the Spirit in the midst as He is today. We are assuming as stubborn an attitude towards Christ as ever Capernaum did. Think of our practical infidelity in spite of our large profession–our Sabbath breaking, pleasure-loving, picture houses open-and crowded, shops open, millions of newspapers sold, our business trickery, common deceit, deified reason, willingness to listen to rationalistic treatment of Divine things. Popular preachers of an attenuated gospel, with a bloodless blessing just tickle your ears. They use the name of Christ, but He is not the crucified Christ, not the mighty Saviour and Redeemer by His shed blood, nor the Son of Man and Son of God of the

Gospels and Epistles. Christ will not thank us for compliments, for naming His name in the same breath as Plato, Aristotle, Browning, etc. He is the supreme unique Man, Son of Man and Son of God. He cannot be classed in the categories of men. To attempt to give Him that place is to insult Him, to pass Him by. Our responsibility is, therefore, so much the greater in assuming the same attitude.

II. Retribution is in the Measure of Responsibility.

Observe that Christ's severest denunciations were pronounced upon those people who stand in a blaze of light and who refuse it. Simply they do not do anything. It is like a bleak rock with the full sunlight pouring upon and around it; it still remains black and bleak. The sailor who, in an awful storm, neglects to lash himself to some fixed post–well the sea does the rest, and he is washed overboard. The soul of man, unless fastened to the Rock Christ, is in awful danger. Human nature, the devil, and circumstances will do the rest! You have only to neglect Christ to have brought down upon you the condemnation of this passage. You say, I do not oppose Christ nor the Bible, nor religion, nor anything that is good. Do you support Christ, the Bible, Christianity? "He that is not with me is against me." There is no neutral position possible.

C. The relative guilt of these cities.

The opportunities differed, though the attitude corresponded. They have the same Judge. He does not fail in practice. *"And shall not the Judge of all the earth do right?"* He takes all into consideration and Sodom, Capernaum, and London will not have the same sentence. Their culpability differs, their guilt is varied, and judgment is according to guilt. Sodom was very guilty, and the judgment was not out of proportion to it. Capernaum was more guilty–Sodom had Lot, Capernaum had Christ, and did not repent, and their guilt is so much greater and their judgment is determined by the measure of guilt. London and the modern cities of Christendom are the most guilty of all. Sodom transgressed against Nature, Capernaum against Revelation, and London is transgressing against Grace.[5] No cities have ever had the opportunities these cities in Christian lands today have had.

Is it possible for a man to live by the side of Niagara until he fails to hear the cataract? Somebody gave evidence of anger at hearing this message. We listen and we listen, and we go out and we do nothing with the message, we do nothing with the Christ declared. It is better that you should never hear the Gospel message, for every time you hear it your responsibility increases. Every time you hear it and do nothing your guilt becomes greater, and you become less sensible to it next time. Woe, woe, woe! If the mighty things had been done in Sodom, and Tyre, and Sidon, they would have repented long ago in sackcloth and ashes. They have not your chance they do not bear your guilt, and your judgment will not be pronounced upon them. The closer a planet comes to the sun the further it plunges into space, and darkness at the other extent of its orbit. The nearer you have come to Christ and the Gospel, the further you are flung at the other extent of your orbit into space and darkness. We can preach the grace of God and the love of God so often, and you can hear it so often and do nothing with is so often, that the only possible thing is to give you a message of judgment. The Gospel we have preached has been soft and has lacked virility and strength, like a picture all light and no shade. There are darker aspects of truth. We speak of the smile of Christ's eyes, and we talk nothing of the deep lines in Christ's brow. He can frown as well as smile. He can speak withering and blistering words as well as words overflowing with tenderness and compassion. We are away back very much further than when the war started [WWI–Author's note]. Then the churches were more full, but the attendance has dropped off–people have soon got used to the war. Life is cheap, Christianity is severely criticized, but God is the same–Christ is the same–the Gospel is the same, and human nature is the same–the conditions of blessing are the same; the way to heaven is

____

5 This message was first given in 1917 at Charlotte Chapel in Edinburgh, then in 1918 at the Metropolitan Tabernacle in London. At the time there was still a prominent Christian majority in the land of Great Britain. Look at it now. Look at America now. We too are transgressing against Grace. But our transgression is deeper, more heinous, more deserving judgment. (EAJ).

the same, the way to hell is the same–the war notwithstanding. There is no new road to heaven by the laying down of life patriotically. There is only one Way, and that is Christ; only one hope, and that is the Cross; we are disposed not to believe it. In the day when the Son of Man comes the world will be caught in pleasures and indifference to things divine and eternal, just giving the Bible, the Church, religion and Christ the go-by. "We find no use for them". In that day it will be more tolerable for Sodom and Gomorrah than for Capernaum, and more tolerable for Capernaum than for the modern cities. There is a day of judgment ahead as surely as there is a God in the universe, and the standard of judgment will be graded, and the severest judgment will be pronounced on those who have had the greatest privileges. What will be the issue where blessing has been received and privileges enjoyed and despised? "Thou shalt be brought down to hell."

I stand in this tragic hour of the world's history deeply soleminsed. A stupendous opportunity is now being given to men which, if missed, will bring down upon them as individuals, as cities, and as nations, the judgment of Almighty God.

The pulpits are in a measure to blame. There is the corroding power of worldliness. Take a bright knife from your table, dig it into the earth in your garden and leave it there. It will soon rust–so will the brightest soul that becomes worldly. We need the Gospel in its strength. We have talked softly. I believe in the Gospel of our Fathers and of this Book, in its terms, in its promises, and in its dark shadows. I believe there is a heaven, and I believe there is a hell. I believe in God and in Christ who is mighty to redeem–and in a present devil, the prince of this world. I believe there is such a thing as right, and certainly there is such a thing as wrong; in holiness to be sought and obtained-and sin. I believe in a way, narrow that leads to life, and a broad way that leads down to destruction–and no other way–no middle truth. Up-down-right-wrong-heaven-hell-God-the devil-holiness-sin. *"Choose ye this day whom you will serve."* You have to say whether for you it shall be light or darkness—Christ or the enemy of your souls. Decide for Christ now. Seek shelter in the precious blood. Get into the place of safety before the storm breaks in all its blast of fury.

HISTORY AND PROPHECY MEET

IN SAFEGUARD (1 Sam. 22:23).

So safe in His keeping by day and by night,
No dangers alarm, and no terrors affright,
Where'er I may be my Lord is near,
I'll trust in His Promise with never a fear.

His Presence sustains me, though rough be the way,
For He is my Comfort, My Rock, and my Stay;
The billows may dash, but He bears me above,
I'll praise Him, and trust Him, and rest in His love.

And so if the furnace I'm called to pass through,
Like the three Hebrew youths, He is there with me too;
He sits and He watches the gold to refine,
The dross to consume His only design.

Though pain and though suffering may oft be my lot,
And friends may prove faithless, yet He changeth not,
Transformed to His image He wants me to be,
That those who reject Him, my Saviour might see.

Dear Lord, keep me ever abiding in Thee,
For then I shall prove Thee my safeguard to be;
And when in the glory I see Thy dear face,
I'll praise and adore Thine Infinite grace.

—E. Cann, Plymouth

SFO Notes

Reading through this sermon brings to mind the powerful prophetic preaching of Jonathan Edwards (1703-1758). In his time, he was America's leading theologian. His fresh Calvinistic preaching brought the Great Awakening to New England. His masterpiece was *"The Freedom of the Will"* (1754). To evangelicals, his most powerful message was *"Sinners in the Hands of an Angry God"* (July 8th, 1741, Enfield Church, New England). Scroggie's sermon above is a close approach to the truths we neglect or even reject in our pulpits today. Without a return to such preaching I see NO HOPE for our nation with the spiritual decline, with moral degradation, and national and global terrorism. We need another GREAT AWAKENING.

9
Spurgeon 1834-1892

Sunday June 29, 1941

Service of witness amid the ruins, the Metropolitan Tabernacle having been destroyed by the Germans on May 11.

Order of Service.

Hymn National Anthem
Prayer
Hymn 1. "All hail the power."
Reading. Isaiah 53.

Spurgeon details

Hymn 20. "Jesus, Loves–".
Prayer
N &O.
Hymn 26. "My hope is built."
Sermon 1 Peter 1:19 *"But the Precious blood of Christ, as of a lamb without blemish and without spot."*
Hymn 43. "There is a fountain."
Bene.

Tabernacle:
Foundation stone laid, August 16, 1859.
Under it–a Bible: Baptist Confession of Faith: a hymn book.
Opened May 18th (Monday), 1861

By a prayer meeting at 7 a.m.
1000 people attending.

First sermon: Monday May 25th, Acts 5:42.
"Daily they ceased not to teach and preach Jesus as the Christ"

Spurgeon, 27 years of age.
Preached here for 30 years: 1861-1891.
13,179 Received in church membership
Membership when he died–5311.
Average of 438 per ann
20,000,000 heard him here.

Not 58 years old when he died.

Colportage, Orphanage, College.
Published a sermon a week for over 62 years
150,000,000 sold, translated into over 25 languages.

While his body lay here, 60,000 persons passed through the
Tabernacle.

M. T. 1898 &1941–destroyed by fire. Future?

10
The Higher Christian Life

"I am crucified with Christ: nevertheless I live; yet not I, but Christ liveth in me: and the life which I now live in the flesh I live by the faith of the Son of God, who loved me, and gave himself for me," (Gal. 2:20).

The great professor Bengle called this text, "the summit and marrow of Christianity." And A. W. Tozer wrote an entire commentary on the deeper Christian life and experience. It is almost impossible to exaggerate the importance of this text for the Spiritual Life. To the degree that we approximate to the Truth of this verse will we experience true Christian life. If you must know any text, let it be this. It is astonishing how many "I's" there can be in a statement and yet that statement be so full of Christianity. In the immediate vicinity of this verse, the Apostle Paul uses the words "I, myself, me" no less than fourteen times!

I. THE DIVINE SOURCE OF THE HIGHER CHRISTIAN LIFE

"The Son of God Who loved me, and gave himself for me."

Two things are immediately obvious–the Son of God versus Saul of Tarsus–God and man in oneness blending.

A. The Son's Atoning Death: *"the Son of God...gave himself."*

1. It Was Virtuous: *"loved."*

The majority of the people in this world are indifferent to us, have no concern for us. But we are loved by Christians. We are loved by God with an everlasting love.

2. It Was Voluntary: *"gave."*

He was not a pawn in a game but a willing sacrifice. (The Puritan Doctrine of the Covenant within the Trinity).

3. It Was Vicarious: *"for me."*

This is missed by so many, but we must grasp this. You can be saved with doubts, but not without faith. He died for you.

B. The Sinner's Appropriating Faith: here we have the place of the sinner.

1. It Was Personal: *"me."*

Yes, He loves the world but that includes you. William Cowper's planned suicide in the Thames failed, "landed through fog on our door!"

Wrote, "God moves in a mysterious way His wonders to perform. He plants his footsteps on the sea and rides upon the storm."

2. It Was Passionate: *"loved."*

A love that demands our response in return. We love Him because He first loved us.

3. It Was Perfect: By strong implication Paul is also saying, "I don't need any other".

We must see the death of Christ as a finished work. Nothing must be added.

II. THE DUAL SPHERE OF THE HIGHER CHRISTIAN LIFE

"the life I now live in the flesh, I live in the faith."

Notice the reference to the two spheres in the text. A Christian always has to function in two spheres: Faith and Flesh.

A. *"In The Flesh"* meaning physical.

This is the medium of its manifestation. *"I live in the flesh."*

A. The Contrast: *"now."*

Not of the present and the past, but his present and the future. He is testifying that a wonderful change has been made. The most important thing is not what you were, but what you are.

B. The Control: *"I live."*

The whole direction of his life was controlled and determined by principle of the Gospel. We do not live fleshly lives but we do live in the flesh. Our natural selves are not destroyed.

2. *"In The Faith"*: meaning Spiritual.

This is the means of its interpretation. *"I live in the faith."*

We have to stay in the environment in which we our spiritual lives can be nourished and maintained by faith in the Son of God. I am to feed on Him, rely absolutely on Him, absorb His faith. The higher Christian life is nothing if it is not a life of faith. How far can your faith go?

III. THE DECLARED SECRET OF THE HIGHER CHRISTIAN LIFE

"I have been crucified." "Christ liveth in me."

The secret is two-fold: his position in Christ and Christ's presence in him. Faith has a recognizable and appropriate and staggering truth: apprehension matched with appropriation.

1. The Believer's Identification with Christ in His Death: *"I am crucified with him."*

It is vital we come to see this Truth—it has always been seen by spiritually minded both ancients and moderns! Way back one of the ancients, Macarius, was questioned as to his emphasis on being dead! Moderns: George Muller, F. J. Huegel who wrote, *Bone of His Bone* is I think one of the best of the modern exponents of this truth. It has to be true of all of us. We must sing with Charles Wesley, "dead to the world." We must see ourselves where God has placed us.

2. Christ's Identification With The Believer In His Life: *"liveth in me."*

How can this be? Since His ascension is He not in heaven? Then how can He live in us? By His Spirit. The Holy Spirit is mentioned no less than 14 times in this short epistle–always in opposition to the flesh. "One must die–which?" No wonder Martin Luther said he so loved this epistle that he was married to it! Luther said, "If anyone knocks at the door of my heart and asks who lives here; I would answer, "Not Martin Luther but Jesus Christ lives here!"

So we see the believer's death to self in Christ and Christ's risen life sovereign in the believer.

SFO Notes

It was hearing this sermon preached that not only challenged and changed my life, but settled my choice of Galatians 2:20 as my life's verse! Eventually, I wrote a whole book on the subject entitled, *Not I But Christ*. Here is just an excerpt from the opening pages:[6] The Content of This Verse. Paul spells this out in no uncertain terms: "A person is justified not by the works of the law but through faith in Jesus Christ...that we might be justified by faith in Christ, and not by doing the works of the law, because no one will be justified by the works of the law. But if, in our effort to be justified in Christ, we ourselves have been found to be sinners, is Christ then a servant of sin? Certainly not! But if I build again the very things that I once tore down, then I demonstrate that I am a transgressor. For through the law I died to the law, so that I might live to God," (Gal. 2:16-19, NRSV). Here, in substance, is the great doctrine of justification by grace through faith. Martin Luther expounded on this passage:

---

6 *Not I But Christ*, Crossway Books, Wheaton, Ill. 1995. Also can be obtained through Olford Ministries Intl. Box 757800, Memphis, TN 38175; 901-757-7977.

> This is the truth of the Gospel. It is also the principle article of all Christian doctrine, wherein the knowledge of all godliness consisteth. Most necessary it is, therefore, that we should know this article well, *teach it unto others, and beat it into their heads continually* [my emphasis].[7]

Read the preceding verses again and follow Paul's argument. Taking his text from Psalm 143:2, Paul interprets what he means by justification. The word *"justified"* occurs four times as a verb in verses 16 and 17 and once as a noun in verse 21. To summarize what Paul teaches in this passage I quote John R. W. Stott:

> Jesus Christ came into the world to live and to die. In His life His obedience to the law was perfect. In His death He suffered for our disobedience. On earth He lived the only life of sinless obedience to the law which has ever been lived. On the cross He died for our law-breaking, since the penalty for disobedience to the law was death. All that is required of us to be justified, therefore, is to acknowledge our sin and helplessness, to repent of our years of self-assertion and self-righteousness, and to put our whole trust and confidence in Jesus Christ to save us. "Faith in Jesus Christ," then, is not intellectual conviction only, but personal commitment. The expression in the middle verse 16 is (literally) "we have believed into *(eis)* Christ Jesus." It is an act of committal, not just assenting to the fact that Jesus lived and died, but running to Him for refuge and calling on Him for mercy.[8]

So justification is not only a legal fact in which we are

---

7 Martin Luther, *A Commentary on St. Paul's Epistle to the Galatians*, rev. and completed translation based on the 'Middleton' edition of the English version of 1575 (Cambridge: James Clarke & Co. Ltd. 1953), p 101.

8 John Stott, *The Message of Galatians*, Downers Grove, Il, InterVarsity Press, 1968, p 62.

declared righteous by a holy God; it is also a transforming experience through a living identification with Christ (v. 17). By union with Christ we are radically transformed; we can no longer go back to our old life, for in Christ we are *"a new creation"* (2 Cor. 5:17).

This brings us to:

The Challenge of This Verse. *"I have been crucified with Christ; it is no longer I who live, but Christ lives in me; and the life which I now live in the flesh I live by faith in the Son of God, who loved me and gave Himself for me,"* (Gal. 2:20). In this matchless statement Paul the apostle encapsulates the gospel of the grace of God. It is **the gospel of the extinguished life**–*"I have been crucified with Christ,"* (Gal. 2:20). We have died to the law. By dying **with** Christ, who died under the law's penalty, we find that all the law's demands were satisfied in Him. They have no more hold on us. Being crucified, moreover, means that we have died to self. The dominating control of the fallen nature has been broken. If we do not understand this, then we are missing something very important. The extinguished life means death to self and sin. In his book, *The Christ-Life for the Self-Life* (addresses delivered mainly at Carnegie Hall, New York, during an ever-memorable week), F. B. Meyer writes:

> The curse of the Christian and of the world is that self is our pivot; it is because Satan made self his pivot that he became a devil. Take heaven from its center in God, and try to center it in self, and you transform heaven into hell. ...The philosophy of the Bible is to do away with self and to make Christ all in all. When dealing with a drunkard I am inclined to say to him, "Be a man." What a fool I am! I am trying to cast out the evil of drink by the evil of self-esteem. If I want to save a man, I must cast out the spirit of self and substitute the Lord Jesus Christ. Alpha, Omega, all in all. But how?...This epistle to the

> Galatians is my battle-axe. Luther used it for justification, but I think it is for sanctification [see Appendix B]. How? By the cross, and by the cross as presented in the epistle to the Galatians. [see 2:20; 3:1; 5:24;6:14]. The apostle tells us in Galatians 1:4, "Jesus Christ...gave Himself for our sins, that He might deliver us from this present evil world, according to the will of God and our Father." He considers the cross in its aspect toward sanctification. He says, "He delivered us from this present evil world." In Romans we have the cross for justification, the putting away of sin; in Galatians for sanctification, the cross standing between me and my past, between me and the world, between me and myself.[9]

So in Galatians 2:20 we have the gospel of the extinguished life. But it is also **the gospel of the relinquished life**–"*It is no longer I who live, but Christ lives in me,*" (Gal. 2:20). No longer is our life self-centered but Christ-centered. By the ministry of the Holy Spirit (as we shall see later) the Lord Jesus lives out His life in us day by day as we maintain total dependence on Him. The apostle says the same thing in his letter to the Romans, exhorting his readers to "*present* [themselves] *to God as being alive from the dead and* [their] *members as instruments of righteousness to God,*" (Rom. 6:13). We do not relinquish ourselves to an enemy, but we present ourselves as a bride to the bridegroom who has wooed and won in us love. As a pastor I have had the privilege of marrying couples times without number. As the two stand before me, I say to the bride, "Will you have this man to be your lawful wedded husband?" She answers in two words, "I will," and they are joined for life. That is the kind of presentation we are thinking of when we speak of the relinquished life. We are saying in effect, "Lord, I am

---

9 F. B. Meyer, *The Christ-Life for the Self-Life*, Chicago, Moody Press, n.d. pp 45-46.

married to You, being alive from the dead, to bring forth fruit unto God. Lord, from now on my language and life are two words: 'I will.'" Every day we must repeat that once-for-all interaction: "I am wholly Yours, Lord. Use me for Your glory." Once again it is **the gospel of the distinguished life**–*"The life which I now live in the flesh I live by faith in the Son of God, who loved me and gave Himself for me,"* (Gal. 2:20). That phrase, *"faith in the Son of God,"* is loaded with rich meaning. Because of our union with Christ crucified and risen, we are *"partakers of the divine nature,"* (2 Pet. 1:4); we actually share with the Son of God the **distinguished life.**

Two aspects of this distinctive life are spelled out for us. As the Son of God, our Lord in His perfect humanity chose to live a **dependent life**. He lived by faith (see John 5:19,30; 6:57; 8:28; and 14:10). We also must live by faith (Rom. 1:17, Heb. 11:6). This life of dependence should be our distinctive. Anything less than this is to live in sin, *"for whatever is not* [of] *faith is sin"* (Rom. 14:23). The other distinctive is that the Son of God lived a **devoted life**. He *"gave Himself for* [us]*"* (Gal. 2:20). That takes in the entire sweep of His life, service, and even His death, in response to the will of His Father. In similar fashion, we are called to the high and holy distinction of yielding ourselves to God as living sacrifices so that we might *"prove what is that good and acceptable and perfect will of God,"* (Rom. 12:1-2). Dependence on God and devotion to God are the marks of divine distinction. Such distinctiveness can be detected anywhere and under any circumstances by a watching world. Out of such a life the streams of living water flow in blessing to others. Certainly this is the testimony of God's people throughout the centuries. Martin Luther experienced this blessing:

> He was a show-piece of discipline and penance, and self-denial and self-torture. "If ever," he said, "a man could be saved by monkery, that

man was I." He had gone to Rome; it was considered to be an act of great merit to climb the Scala Sancta, the great sacred stairway, on hands and knees. He toiled upwards seeking that merit that he might win; and suddenly there came to him the voice from heaven: *"The just shall live by faith."* The life at peace with God was not to be attained by this futile, never-ending, ever-defeated effort; it could only be had by casting himself on the love and mercy of God as Jesus Christ has revealed them to men. It is when a man gives up the struggle which the pride of self thinks it can win, but must ever lose, and when he abandons himself to the forgiving love of God that peace must come.[10]

The blessing that flowed from Luther's life changed the face of Europe and, ultimately, the fate of millions. John Wesley was one of those affected. His was a cultured mind, matched only by his spiritual sensitivity, servant attitude, and social concern. But he was a discouraged man as he returned to England from Savannah, Georgia. He had encountered great problems in his attempt to deal with the colonists in the New World. Indeed, these outward and inward battles brought him to doubt his own acceptability before the God he loved and served. In this frame of mind he went one evening–most reluctantly–to a meeting where Luther's "Preface to the Epistle to the Romans" was read. During the reading, Wesley's "heart was strangely warmed." He recorded in his journal:

> I felt I did trust in Christ alone for salvation; and an assurance was given to me that he had taken away my sins, even mine, and saved me from *"the law of sin and death."*[11]

---

10 William Barclay, *The Letters to the Galatians and Ephesians*, The Daily Study Bible (Edinburgh: St. Andrew Press, 1959), pp 23-24.

11 Percy L. Parker, ed., *Journals of John Wesley* (Chicago: Moody Press, 1974), p 64.

A SAMPLE OF DR. SCROGGIE'S ITINERARY MINISTRY

Armed with this message of union with Christ in His death and resurrection, John Wesley embarked on forty years of ministry that beggars description. So mightily did the Spirit of God use him that revivals blazed in England and America throughout the eighteenth and nineteenth centuries, and the course of history was changed.

- C. C. (Charlotte Chapel in Edinburgh) 10/3/20
- London Zion College 5/10/21
- Sunderland 5/15/21
- Ed. Convention 6/23/22
- Keswick 7/18/22
- Glasgow Cambuslang 1/14/23
- Sunderland (Bethesada Free Church) 4/27/23
- Ridgelands 11/28/23
- Met. Tab. (The Metropolitan Tabernacle) 11/29/23
- Oxford 2/2/24
- Philadelphia 12/6/24
- Ottowa 6/26/24
- Gull Lake 7/3/24
- Eaglesmere 7/9/24
- Hamilton 8/6/24
- Toronto 8/10/24
- Elgin Hse 8/19/24
- Winnipeg 9/5/24
- Cambuslang 2/22/25
- Rossie Priory Aug '25
- Shetland Aug '25
- C. C. 11/22/25
- Crieff 12/10/26
- St. George's Edinburgh 2/3/27
- Dumfries 4/18/27
- Bath 5/5/27
- Wellington 10/6/27
- Cambridge 01/24/28
- Stoneybrook 7/18/28
- Philadelphia 7/27/28
- Chicago 7/29/28
- Chicago 8/1/28
- Toronto Canada 8/12/28
- Strong Brook 8/23/28
- Belfast y.m.c.a. 3/1/28
- Stoneybrook 7/19/28
- Dundee Scotland 10/31/28
- Paisley 11/25/28
- Belfast y.m.c.a. 2/17/29
- Liverpool 4/24/29
- Dublin St. Baptist Edinburgh 5/26/29
- Morningside Baptist 3/23/30
- Swanwich 4/27/30
- Christ Church 5/25/30
- Portstewart North Ireland 6/29/30
- Wallesley 7/20/30
- Folkestone 10/16/30
- Dublin 11/20/30
- C. C. 2/14/32
- Johannesburg 5/4/32
- Pretoria 5/15/32
- Bulawayo 5/20/32
- Durban 6/28/32
- Edinburgh Fountain Hall 12/18/32
- Harwick 2/19/33
- Strathpeffer 9/27/33
- Norwood 10/15/33

- Auchland N. Z. 12/11/33
- Auckland y.m.c.a. 5/1/34
- Sydney N. S. W. 6/13/34
- Brisbane 7/13/34
- Adelaide 8/17/34
- Melbourne 9/30/34
- Geelong 10/14/34
- Ballarat 11/11/34
- Hobart 12/1/34
- Barnet 5/2/35
- C. C. 6/19/35
- Frogal 10/14/35
- Highbury Quandrant 10/30/35
- Walthamston 11/14/35
- Sunderland 11/24/35
- Newcastle 12/8/35
- C. C. 12/22/35
- Ealing 01/29/36
- Portsmouth 2/12/36
- Worthing 6/28/36
- Met. Tab. Spurgeon's 7/19/36
- Torquay 9/28/36
- Vancouver 10/28/36
- Victoria B. C. 11/6/36
- Seattle 11/27/36
- Bellingham 12/16/36
- Vancouver 12/30/36
- Portland 01/10/37
- Berkeley Calif. 01/19/37
- Pasadena 2/16/37
- Hollywood 2/23/37
- San Diego 3/24/37
- Long Beach 4/11/37
- Long Beach 4/12-13/37
- Denver 4/18/37
- Chicago 5/4/37
- Buffalo 5/9/37
- Portland 6/1/37
- Muskoka 7/14/37
- Oakland Calif. 7/31/37
- Montrose Pa 8/5/37
- N. Z. Keswick 8/12/37
- New Jersey Keswick 8/14/37
- New York First Baptist 8/15/37
- Winona Lake 8/20/37
- Bournemouth 9/20/37
- Met. Tab. 9/29/37
- Manchester 10/5/37
- Portsmouth 10/24/37
- Met. Tab. 2/13/38
- St. Paul's Portman Sq. 2/15/38
- Met. Tab. 2/20/38
- Croydin Crusaders 6/3/38
- Beckinham 10/4/38
- Minister Wives 01/13/39
- E.G.M. Annual 01/31/39
- Ashtead Camp 01/6/42
- St. Andrews Edinburgh 8/2/42
- Oxford 4/11/43
- Cambridge 10/26/44
- Epsom 11/17/46
- Glasgow Lyric Theatre 6/3/46
- Glasgow 6/11/46
- Westminster Chapel 8/25/46
- Ealing Crusaders 4/30/49
- Missionary School of Medicine 3/14/50
- Wellesley Fellowship 3/25/50
- Civil Service C. U. Orange St. 4/13/50

11
CHRISTIAN PRODUCTIVENESS

> *"The same day went Jesus out of the house, and sat by the sea side. And great multitudes were gathered together unto him, so that he went into a ship, and sat; and the whole multitude stood on the shore. And he spake many things unto them in parables, saying, 'Behold, a sower went forth to sow; And when he sowed, some seeds fell by the way side, and the fowls came and devoured them up: Some fell upon stony places, where they had not much earth: and forthwith they sprung up, because they had no deepness of earth: And when the sun was up, they were scorched; and because they had no root, they withered away. And some fell among thorns; and the thorns sprung up, and choked them: But other fell into good ground, and brought forth fruit, some an hundredfold, some sixtyfold, some thirty-fold. Who hath ears to hear, let him hear.'"* (Matt. 13:1-9 Also texts Matt. 25:14-27 and Luke 19:12-23).

In Matthew 13 verse eight we read, *"Some 100 fold, some 60 and some 30."* In Mark four verse eight it says, *"Some thirty, some sixty and some an hundred."* In Luke chapter eight verse eight it just says, *"one hundred fold."* It will be well for us to observe the variations in these records. Matthew shows a diminishing order, Mark shows an increasing order, while Luke just says, *"one hundred fold"*—the maximum. It is probable that Christ spoke this parable quite frequently, and, if so, would account for the varying order of the reports. Let us now look at three matters of tremendous importance with relationship to Christian fruitfulness.

I. THE CONDITIONS OF IT.
II. THE DEGREES OF IT.
III. THE REWARDS OF IT.

I. THE CONDITIONS OF FRUITFULNESS.

If the seed is to be productive, it is by reason of the fitness of the soil into which it falls. Unlike the wayside, the soil must be soft and not hard; unlike the rocky place, it must be deep and not shallow; and unlike the thorny ground, it must be clean and not dirty. We see, then, that fruitfulness is dependent upon the attitude of the soul to the Word, as the Word is the seed, and the soul is the soil. The rocky place hearer is not productive, because of his impulsiveness. The thorny place hearer is not productive, because of his indulgence. The impulsive are superficial, and the indulgent are pre-occupied. In this parable our Lord attributes the insensibility to the devil, the superficiality to the world, and the self-indulgence to the flesh. But in the good soil we see the influence of good. He hears and takes, and, unlike the thorny ground hearer, he keeps. In order that there be Christian productiveness, there must be Reflection on the Word of Life. (The wayside hearer does not do that). There must be Reception of the Word of Life. (The rocky place hearer does not receive). There must be Retention of the Word of Life. (The thorny ground hearer does not hold what it takes).

II. THE DEGREES OF FRUITFULNESS.

Our Lord teaches that in the case of the good soil there are degrees of fruitfulness. Has this ever puzzled us? Why degrees? Should there be such, must there be such, seeing that all the soil is good? For the answer we must turn to nature. All good soil is not equally good. These natural facts appear in the spiritual realm, and depend on two things–Opportunity and Fidelity. These two principles are richly illustrated by the other two parables–the one of the Talents, and that of the Pound.

In the parable of the Talents it is the Christian's ability that is in view; but in the parable of the Pound it is his integrity.

A. Fruitfulness According to Ability.

In this parable (Matt. 25:14-30) we see that the servants were given, respectively, five, two, and one talent. On what principle were the talents given? Each according to his ability. So we must distinguish between the ability and the talents. They had the ability before they were given the talents, and the gifts were determined by their ability. When we speak of a talented person, we speak of his ability, but in the parable the talents and ability are different. The man of rich ability is given many opportunities—five talents; the man of average ability is given some opportunities—two talents; and the man of poor ability is given, at least, one talent. We are not responsible for our abilities, but for our opportunities. We cannot increase our ability, as we are born with that, and it is our capital. We cannot increase our ability, but only put it out to use. This is the case where all the soil is good, but not equally good, as some have genius, some average and some poor ability. So, then, all the soil cannot be equally productive, and therefore there are degrees of fruitfulness. This is vitally and tremendously important, and for want of recognizing it we go astray. In the second parable we see

B. Fruitfulness According to Fidelity.

This parable (Luke 19:12-27) differs from the first, as each was on an equal standing, and what each did with his depended not upon his ability but upon his fidelity. What, then, does the Pound represent? That is not quite so easy to determine, but it would appear that Grace is at the foundation. God has not equipped us all in the same way in the matter of spiritual grace. Each has that Pound, and has what the apostle calls the common salvation. In the case of the Pound, there is no respect or persons, and all is dealt out impartially. The grace given a man for his probationary life here is the only gift which each of us has. Here we all start on the same plane. The great saints of history began with the pound, neither more nor less, and the least of saints have the same pound. We see, then, that some thirty, sixty, and one hundred fold is inevitable, and there is no reflection upon the fruits of the producers. Now this becomes clearer when we consider finally

3. THE REWARD OF FRUITFULNESS.

These rewards are made according to principle and measure; as to principle, they are righteous, and as to measure, they are graded. Do not imagine for one moment that at the Judgment everyone will be on the same level and judgment will be given out equally to all. The gifts given are varied–with glorious opportunities to all. The higher rewards are not given to the more richly gifted, as such, as we would feel that was unfair, and we can never attribute anything unfair to God. Now suppose each of these persons in the service of Christ used his talents to the utmost. The first has large opportunities, the third has poor opportunities, and the second has average opportunities. Are rewards going to be dealt out the same to all? NO. But according to the measure of what we have done with what has been given us. Where different endowments and opportunities are improved to the limit of ability, notwithstanding that the results are varied, the rewards are the same. The man that had five talents got ten, and the man with two got four. Both were rewarded the same–*"Good, faithful servant."* He did all he could with what he had. We may not have the mind of Paul, or the flash and power of Luther, or Wesley, or Whitefield, but no power will get anyone more, when rewards are given out, than you will get. Rewards as to principle are on a basis of righteousness–God is just. Then the measure is graded. Did the two who traded get the same as the one who did nothing? Oh, no. Varying industry will be variously rewarded. That is fair. There are Christians who are bringing forth one hundred fold, and are doing their best. There are those who are bringing forth sixty fold and thirty fold, and are doing their best–they can do no more. But the worst thing conceivable is that the hundred fold should despise and criticize the thirty fold. But in the case of the pound, each of us has eternal life, the Holy Spirit; and none have any advantage over another.

So two great lessons emerge:

1st –Our Ability, If Faithfully Used, Will Be Rewarded To Eternal Gain.

2nd –That Lack Of Loyalty Will Result In Eternal Loss Of Reward.

In closing, let me give you this illustration:

Two people get converted at gospel outreach, or in a church. They are Christ's. They have received a call, and go out and start the Christian life. One, without any hesitation or compromise, strikes the trail, and follows Christ, coming into a place of prominence and power in the church. He is called on to suffer for his convictions. The other cannot face the music, and is not prepared to pay the price. He compromises and slips back into the world, and becomes neither black nor white, but grey. Are they going to be rewarded equally on the basis of their talents? The second is saved, but *"so as by fire."* This is what the backslider may expect at the Judgment Seat of Christ. Don't let us make any mistake, there is no levelling up at the finish; we will be rewarded be according to what we have done with our pound here. If you backslide, there will be no reward. You did not do all you could have done with your pound.

Jesus, confirm my heart's desire
To work, and speak and think for Thee:
Still let me guard the holy fire,
And stir up Thy gift in me;

Ready for all Thy perfect will,
My acts of faith and love repeat,
Till death, Thine endless mercies seal,
And make the sacrifice complete.

SFO Notes

"Saved, yet as through fire" (2 Cor. 3:15). This reference within the nuance of its context opens up a whole line of teaching which is barely preached from our pulpits today; hence this SIDE BAR. It has to do with THE JUDGMENT SEAT OF CHRIST for all believers. As sinners we were judged at the cross once and for all (Isa. 53:6,9; 2 Cor. 5:21). As sons we are being judge day by day (Heb. 12:5-11). As saints we will be judged at the Bema ("Tribunal") in a coming day, (2 Cor. 5:10-11). In these two verses, Paul is thinking primarily, if not exclusively, of the Christian's obligation to give an account of himself (Rom. 14:12). Study also 1 Corinthians 3 in full. Note: we shall be rewarded if we have lived and served to the glory of God under the control of the Spirit; and yet not all verdicts will be comforting. The believer may *"suffer loss"* (1 Cor. 3:15) by forfeiting Christ's praise or by losing his reward. Here is truth that must be preached in these days of careless and even callous living.

12
Travelling by the Long Road[12]

"And it came to pass when Pharaoh had let the people go, that God led them not through the way of the land of the Philistines, although that was near; for God said, Lest peradventure the people repent when they see war and then return to Egypt: but God led the people about, through the way of the wilderness of the Red Sea," (Ex. 13:17-18).

In a world like this, most people are conscious of the difficulty of the way; and Christians are by no means excluded. Those of us who profess the name of Christ have not only the difficulties to face which are common to all men, but also difficulties which arise from our profession of Christ. The Lord has not promised to those who believe, a programme without problems; but He has promised to be with us in our difficulties, and to bring us through. As, therefore, we reflect upon the past, and anticipate the future, it will be well if we look at our problem in the light of God's purpose. At first sight it strikes us as strange that God should have chosen this way for Israel, although a reason is given. Was there no alternative to the long way? Were there not difficulties either way, and might they not have faced the difficulty of the shorter route? Let us then think of their problem and our own together, and consider first:

---

12 This message by Graham Scroggie is one of his most famous and beloved. It touched the hearts of more listeners than any other of his sermons. And in his personal papers are several hand written letters by church members who heard the message and whose lives were touched by it. It is a message of hope and its remarkable insights are needed greatly today. EAJ

I. THE PROVIDENCE OF THE LONG ROAD.

The shortest way may not be the surest. Short cuts to the goal are often dangerous cuts. There may be a very real peril in a cross-country track.

True Sense of Values

From Egypt to Canaan was about a week's journey, yet the Israelites were led 200 miles out of the course, and took forty years to get into the Land, entering it from the east instead of from the west. Probably the Israelites did not regard the route as providential, yet events proved that it was, and for at least three reasons. First, was their inability quickly to appreciate the blessings of the Land. These people had been told of the value of Palestine agriculturally, geographically, and historically, but had they entered it in about a week after leaving Egypt, it would have been without any due sense of their privilege. Great blessings easily come by are generally little thought of. It is the man who does not earn his wealth who often squanders it. The things we value most are the things which have cost us most. We should never pray that we may be easily enriched, for it is not the gold which drops from the sky which we value, but that which we dig from the earth. The long road teaches us to appreciate what we find at the end of it.

In the second place, this way was providential for the Israelites because of their inability to resolutely overcome the resistance of the foe. The Philistines were a strong and warlike people, and any attempt on the part of Israel to enter the land from their side of it would have provoked the utmost hostility, and certainly led to Israel's discomfiture. The people's experience in Egypt had not prepared them for war, and, humanly speaking, the short road would have meant utter destruction. I doubt not that for years God has been leading many of His people out of the path of some enemies, and in this way He has been answering the prayer, *"Lead us not into temptation."* Through the divine mercy we are victorious to-day over temptations which would have crushed us twenty, or ten, or even five years ago. Then we were not ready, but now we are, but it has been by means of the long road.

No Easy Victories

Let us never pray for easy victories. There are no short cuts to conquest. Bloodless battles in this warfare decide nothing—they are generally evasions. For lasting results there must be costly preparation, and for this the long road is needed. We have never seen the last or the worst of our enemies until death is destroyed (1. Cor. 15:26).

In the third place, the Israelites needed the long way because of their inability to shoulder the responsibility of government all at once. In Egypt they had been a horde of slaves, but in Canaan they were to be a properly constituted and well-organized nation. Such a change could not be wrought in a week. Nations are not made in a day. They have small beginnings, as on the Mayflower, and grow strong and able by failure and success, sorrow and joy, suffering and struggle, until, as in the American States today, they can shoulder an estimable share of the world's load. And this is true also of the individual. The burden is suited to the back while the back is being strengthened for heavier burdens. Sometimes we crave great responsibilities, for a position of trust and power, little knowing that such would be our ruin. Responsibility belongs only to experience, and we can gain but little experience in the short road. There are no cross-country cuts to Empire. Even Christ came to that by way of the wilderness. Travail must precede birth. Struggle must go before sovereignty. Training must be undergone in order to accomplish anything worthwhile. Only the long road brings us to Canaan. We should thank God, therefore, for the detours in our road, for the circuitous route, for the wilderness way which saves us from irrecoverable defeat at the beginning.

And now let us think of

II. THE NECESSITY FOR THE LONG ROAD.

This must be evident to us in what has already been said, but we must consider the matter from other angles.

A. Such a road as this is necessary for the purpose of self-discovery.

The Israelites would have discovered themselves too late

had they gone to Canaan by the short road, for they would not have proved their utter weakness and sinfulness, and consequently would have undertaken tasks for which they were not fit, and failing, would have run away. It is not the picnic which tests us, but the fatiguing journey; not the stroll by the river, but the march through the desert. It is as necessary a part of our education to learn what we are not, and cannot do, as to know what we are, and can do. God's long road for us is always shorter than our experience finds it to be. At the end of two years, travelling by Sinai, the Israelites should have been in the land, but they took forty years to get there. Through these years they were making one long discovery of their exceeding sinfulness. God says that they tempted and provoked Him ten times. Each of us must discover his unworthiness if we would be any use to God, but how long we take to do it is a matter for ourselves. Every year unnecessarily spent in the desert is a year less of joy in the Land. "Too late," at the age of thirty-two says Augustine, "too late I learned to love Thee, O Thou Beauty of Ancient Days: too late I learned to love Thee."

Then,

B. Such a road as this is necessary for the exercise of moral discipline.

The real reason for the long road lay, not in the Philistines, but in the Israelites themselves. They had not learned to obey, nor to endure; and they were deficient in courage and faith. As yet they were still in their moral and spiritual infancy, and therefore were unfit for the sphere and service of the mature. So, our life is our school. Every mile has its lesson, and every minute its message. When Satan tempts us, God tests us. Failure is a challenge to courage. Difficulty is an opportunity for faith. Privation and disappointment are calls for endurance.

Purpose of Discipline

Our curriculum is severe according to the value of the degree we would take. Discipline is the business of life, and has for its end moral perfection. The cross is our friend and not our enemy. Where there is no difficulty, there is no deliverance.

Where there is no depression, there is no rapture. No sense of need means no cry to God. No dark night means no blazing stars. The wilderness and the long road are our friends.

Then, again

(iii) Such a road is necessary for the opportunity of military training.

The Israelites were not used to arms, and had never fought a battle; they were, therefore, no match for the Philistines and Anakim, so God sent them into the wilderness to learn. Their tests were graded and their progress was gradual.

This is always God's way with His people. He does not send us to the front-line trenches to begin with, but He sends us first to camp, then to the base, then forward a little to observe, and so gradually on to life's big battles, and to the great victories, if only we are faithful. It will be well then if we see that the circuitous route is providential and necessary; that, indeed, by no other way can we arrive at the appointed goal.

But we should not suppose that such a way as this is hard necessity only. There is tenderness in God's discipline of us. There is glory in the struggle. Seeming impoverishment may be great enrichment. We should not be hasty in our judgments, but should take the long view of the difficult way.

Consider, then in conclusion, some of

III. THE COMPENSATIONS OF THE LONG ROAD.

One of these is:

C. Divine companionship and guidance.

We are not alone on this road—God is with us. Twice in our text it is said, *"God led them."* The path on which God is, must be the best way. The shortest journey without Him will be long, and the longest with Him will be short. He does not send us "round about," but leads us; and so the way will not be unnecessarily long. The most difficult journey is made easy when the companionship is right.

When Christ is with us, the desert will blossom as the rose. He Himself did not take the short way, though He was tempted so to do. The devil bade Him attain at once to sovereignty, but the price was the abandonment of faith and reason and conscience. But Christ said "No," and took the long road by Calvary. To take the short cut will be to miss Him, and also to miss the goal.

The Lord Jesus needed companionship once, and said to His apostles, *"Let us go hence."* Now, we need companionship, and should say, as Moses did, *"If Thy presence go not with me, carry me not up hence."* And He will say to us, as He did to Moses, *"My presence shall go with thee, and I will give thee rest."* Surely this companionship and guidance will make the long road gloriously worthwhile.

Bounteous Provision
Another compensation is:

B. Divine provision.
Water from the rock and bread from heaven were given to the travellers. God not only leads us, but He also feeds us.

The twenty-third Psalm is full of meaning in this connection. "The Lord is my Shepherd, I shall not want" —I shall not want rest (v.2), or guidance (2,3), or grace (3), or companionship or protection (4), or food, or joy, or drink (5), or anything, either in this life or in the life to come (6). In this light, the long road loses its terrors; in the wilderness waters break out, and streams in the desert; the parched ground becomes a pool, and the thirsty land becomes springs of water. With such companionship and provision we can sing our song in the night.

But this is by no means all the compensation of the long road. It is there that we receive also:

C. Divine unveiling.
It was in the wilderness that the Israelites received the revelation of God's will for them, and of their way of approach to Him in the law, the tabernacle, the priesthood, and the offerings. There the people were not only led and fed, but also taught.

How true it is that "knowledge by suffering entereth." Character is the reward of discipline. The long road took Ezekiel to the Chebar, but there he was given the Temple vision. The long road took Paul to a Roman prison, but there he saw divine things more fully and clearly then ever he had seen them before, and what he saw he has shown us in Ephesians and Colossians. The long road took John to the Island of Patmos, but there the gates of the future were opened to him, and he saw the triumph of Calvary in the universal Kingdom of Christ. The long road took Bunyan to Bedford jail, but from there he has enriched the whole Church of God.

The whole story can never be told. When the saints of all the ages bear their final witness, they will declare with one voice that the long road was the right road. Then, let us foot it, not grudgingly but gladly, not with limping feet but with lilting heart, not with reluctant submission but with grateful acquiescence. If we do this, our weights will be transfigured into wings, and our handicaps will become stepping-stones to glory.[13]

SFO Notes

The journey from Egypt to Canaan is the greatest Bible illustration of our spiritual journey from bondage to blessing taught in such passages as Romans chapters 6-8, and other epistles. As you read and work on this sermon–fill in the actual verses or passages that Dr. Scroggie is referring to. Remember that the whole generation that left Egypt never entered Canaan! There were two exceptions: Joshua and Caleb. Why was this? An important passage to study in this connection is Hebrews 4. Read it carefully and notice particularly verse 2c.

---

13 One must sit back and reflect upon this message for its truths are timeless. One must also be aware that this sermon was given by a man who was known for living a life of holiness. When Dr. Scroggie delivered this message he had the Spirit of God upon him in a powerful anointing; an anointing that is sadly as absent from our pulpits today as holiness is out of them. EAJ